The End of Old America

SECOND EDITION

The End of Old America

SECOND EDITION

Thomas G. Reed

LAURUS BOOKS

Unless otherwise specified, all Scripture quotations are from the **King James Version of the Holy Bible (KJV)**, which is available in the Public Domain.

The End of Old America

SECOND EDITION

By Thomas G. Reed

Paperback Book: ISBN: 978-1-957528-08-3
Mobi (Kindle): ISBN: 978-1-957528-09-0

Cover design and illustration by Grace Metzger Forrest
Cover Photo by Jeremy Bishop on Unsplash

Published by LAURUS BOOKS

Printed in the United States of America

LAURUS BOOKS
www.TheLaurusCompany.com

This book may be ordered in paperback version from TheLaurusCompany.com, Amazon.com and most other retailers around the world. Also available in formats for electronic readers from their respective stores.

Acknowledgements

I wish to express my appreciation to
Mr. Perry Ennis
who was kind enough
to put me in contact with
a godsend—
Mrs. Nancy E Williams,
my wonderful editor and publisher.

Table of Contents

Introduction

T*he End of Old America* ***SECOND EDITION*** explores the loss of a way of life in the America we grew up in. It's a sobering story because, today, it is so hard to find a remnant of the traditions of our Founding Fathers, the old ways of honor, duty, and love for others.

Personal integrity and the Golden Rule seem relics of our past. What has happened to America? What has happened to us? After all, isn't this America, the shining city on a hill, a beacon of hope for the beleaguered masses of downtrodden humanity?

Ironically, many of us here in the shining city have lost our own hope in the future of our beloved country, our economic model, and our founding faith. Many are unable, or afraid, to admit that the American Eagle is struggling to maintain her flight and will eventually fall from her perch of international power and prominence.

There is more sad news. America's economic model appears headed for failure, too, and is well on the way already. These tragedies are compounded by the apostasy of much of mainline Christianity, so diluted with worldliness that our religion is relatively ineffective in the struggles against immorality in America.

The demise of America and her foundational institutions is not by accident or default. It has been and continues to be a planned program to destroy a country, her way of life, and her very structure, by a movement that is anathema to all that Christian conservatives hold dear. The movement is humanism, and its pervasive tentacles (e.g., liberalism, socialism, communism, feminism, progressivism, etc.) are determined to destroy or at least humble us into submission to the humanists' globalist goals.

The End of Old America SECOND EDITION examines the death grip that humanism has on America, her mode of commerce, and her religious structures. Unfortunately, we have all been affected by the humanistic mix in our culture, so much so that the future of our country, our economy, our faith, and freedoms are at stake.

Enemies of the land that we love are many, and over the years, they have waged a successful revolution against all that was the old America. Now, our enemies hold the higher ground in the struggle for uncontested power. The situation is doomed to get worse.

The same forces that crept in and stole our way of life yesterday are still at work today. Humanists are so deeply embedded in America's power structures that they are stronger than ever, more determined than ever to "fundamentally transform" the United States of America into a neutered lapdog of the New World Order.

America's economic model is viewed by those of the humanist persuasion as the cause of poverty and the world's disparity in the distribution of wealth. As a result, when the humanists came into power in the last century, they handcuffed capitalism with an array of rules, regulations, and illegal taxations, on its way to the gallows of total socialist strangulation.

The End of Old America ***SECOND EDITION*** takes a long look at capitalism, her synthesis with socialism, and her eventual fall. As even a casual observer of politics and economics has seen, capitalism is well on its way to total submission to the wishes of liberal socialists. Her end may very well be near.

Sadly, much of mainline Christianity in America is unaware of its ineffectiveness, too absorbed with doctrines of self-improvement, prosperity, and fitting in. Sure, American religion remains "churchy," but it displays only a form of godliness instead of the actual manifestation of holiness itself. Because the church couches impurity instead of railing against it, the power of God to transform lives is noticeably absent. As a result, America's founding faith has failed to stem the tidal wave of immorality flooding our country. This inability of the church to counter the effects of humanism in our lives has arguably led to the loss of the culture war.

Rather than making converts out of atheistic humanists, the opposite has happened. Humanism has invaded the church and had a devastating impact on how we live and how we treat people in America. As we shall see, humanism is a religion, and its advocates actively wage holy war against all who oppose them, with a zeal unmatched by their counterparts in modern-day Christianity. Because the war for the very soul of America is spiritual, we feel that it must be fought on a spiritual plane. Shouldn't we reform ourselves and hope and pray for a national reformation? Before addressing that question, we must take a comprehensive look at the doctrines of religious humanism and its effects on America. Sadly, the demise of American values and America's prominence in the world serves as the perfect illustration of the decline of Earth's entire civilization, a downward spiral toward the End of Time, as we now know it. ■

Chapter 1
A Troubled Country

America is our home, the land we love and hold dear. This country was at one time a symbol of hope for the entire world, a benevolent force with the potential to spread prosperity, freedom, and enriching Christian values throughout mankind.

The colonists—our forefathers—came to America seeking freedom. They fled the selfish, all-powerful dictates of monarchs and clergy. They risked life and limb to be free from church and state planners, free to worship as they pleased, to make their own plans, use their own ingenuity, make their own choices. Through Herculean effort and sacrifice they achieved freedom, and for centuries, they kept it.

The simple word "Americana" evokes a heartwarming and inspiring vision of a vast and glorious land, rich in both opportunity and tradition. When we think of Americana we see the farmer admiring his golden fields of wheat, rippling in the light of the setting sun after a hard but honest day's work. We hear the school bell ringing and see the Stars and

Stripes running up the schoolhouse flag pole as the children stand in attendance with their hands on their hearts. We envision the extended family gathering around the Thanksgiving table set for a feast. We picture the low brick buildings lining Main Street in a quaint small town, where everyone knows their neighbors, and no one has to lock their doors. Where kids get on their bikes in the morning and don't come home 'til suppertime, and no one need worry for their safety.

When we were young, elders were cherished, respected, and cared for. No one laughed at the word "manners." People aimed to be polite, helpful, and chivalrous. Communities banded together to help anyone in need. We had never heard of the phrase "road rage." No one could even imagine kneeling during our national anthem. We bore true allegiance to our flag. In short, we were patriots, and our America was the shining city on a hill, a refuge for the beleaguered masses of downtrodden humanity.

America is the mighty land built on the traditions of our Founding Fathers, the Judeo-Christian value set, and the Golden Rule. It is the champion of freedom, here and abroad. It is the land of the industrious, the land of honor, duty, and love for our fellow man. Personal integrity is paramount. Our word is our bond. We are the people who brought the world magnificent documents such as the Declaration of Independence, the Constitution, and the Bill of Rights.

For nearly 150 years, the salt of Christian belief and behavior seasoned our society, augmenting every aspect of our lives. At one time, our government, our educational system, our culture, and our worldview all reflected the teachings of God's Holy Word. While Americans are human, and therefore fallible, as a rule, morality prevailed, and with it, freedom and liberty triumphed.

Unfortunately, we must use the past tense to describe that country. That America is no more.

In spite of our nation's godly heritage, over the past several decades, Christian ethics have lost their positive influence on the social and cultural aspects of American life. Traditional America has silently slid into the salvage yards of obsolescence. A new America has subtly and slyly emerged, dominated by liberal elites and ignorant, self-serving masses who ask not what they can do for their country, but what their country can do for them.

In a *Chicago Tribune* column, March 15, 2016, Rosemary Warschawski wrote, "Liberals often do not recognize the genius of the American Experiment. Based more closely than any other country known so far on the Judeo-Christian principle of individual liberty, coupled with individual responsibility, America has been a light to the nations. Warts and all, it has provided opportunity to the masses, lifted more people out of poverty and disease, and opened a pathway to the top for anyone willing to work hard and sacrifice."

As values disintegrate, we shred the fabric of our society. We pave the way for the immoral majority to capture our country at the voting booth. And when this shameless majority prevails at election time, activist liberal judges are not far behind. Herald the beginning of tyranny and the end of freedom.

Yes, freedom itself is now an endangered species. Freedom equals responsibility. Self-rule is only effective when the "self" is able and willing to behave responsibly. Freedom requires moral behavior and individual constraints. An unholy, undisciplined, self-serving populace cannot effectively govern a country. Absent the Christian code of ethics and a basic sense of duty and honor, humanist relativism takes over. The gates are flung wide for the liberal takeover, with their socialist agenda. As they gleefully grab the reins, they strip us of our choices, our responsibility, and most of all, our freedom.

After decades of liberalism and moral decay, "we the people" are no longer truly free. Much like Europe under monarchs or fascist/communist dictatorships, America now places constraints on the individual's right to plan his own life or distribute his resources as he sees fit. Instead, the liberals in both parties intend to do our thinking for us. They confiscate our earnings and make their own decisions about who deserves to benefit from our labor. In this new America, the state has become the benefactor and the decision-maker, taking on god-like status.

Accountability and Responsibility

When the state steps in and does our thinking, personal accountability and responsibility are lost. If man is not free to choose between good and evil, then he is not responsible for his actions. It is clear that in today's new America, taking responsibility for one's own success has become a thing of the past. Citizens must be cared for, cradle to grave: socially, financially and spiritually.

The American focus has turned to special-interest groups, who claim extraordinary privileges, without lifting a finger to earn them. Members of these groups feel they are entitled to these privileges. The special rights, special treatment, and special benefits they demand invariably infringe on the rights and freedoms of those who are unwilling or unable to claim this disproportionate position of consideration and power. Those with traditional values and pride in their own efforts are now members of a shrinking minority, increasingly ostracized and ignored by their own government.

Traditional Americans would never stoop so low as to claim privilege above other members of society. As Rosemary Warschawski pointed out, we have made victims out of minorities, reinforcing the fallacy that they need our help because they can't make it on their own. That philosophy—a liberal philosophy—is in itself a form of bigotry. We are in favor of helping all citizens rise to their highest potential, but we are not in favor of lowering our country's standards for them. As Ms. Warschawski said, "I want to pay our fair share to the government as long as it goes to the common good. I want roads, schools, law enforcement, and national security. But I don't want to pay for other people's poor choices, passivity, or lifestyles."

The New America

John Adams said, "Our Constitution is made only for a moral and religious people. It is wholly inadequate to the government of any other … The principles of democracy are as easily corrupted as human nature is corrupted." Our first President, George Washington, added, "Of all the dispositions and habits that lead to political prosperity, religion, and morality are indispensable supports … Where is the security for property, for reputation, for life, if the sense of religious obligation deserts the oaths which are the instruments of investigation in the courts of justice?"

America is no longer a moral and religious people, so what has become of our Constitution? It has been maligned and distorted by liberal judges who make false interpretations and prejudiced misapplications.

Our distinguished and lofty documents of freedom and justice have been wasted on the unscrupulous liberal mob that now rewrites the law to further their selfish agenda. This mob is given free rein, as the media minimizes or ignores their insidious and often violent or destructive acts.

As Samuel Adams pointed out, "It is not possible that any state should long remain free where virtue is not supremely honored." While remnants of American values and traditions survive, they are imprisoned and enslaved within the invisible walls of the liberals' fortress. In other words, there are now two Americas. One is in power, and the other, the traditional, is tucked silently away, under guard.

In this new America, Christian morals are no longer nurtured or even accepted. Deception is on steroids. An apathetic Self has become our god. Those of us with values, standards, and a sense of responsibility are maligned. Many people are so desensitized to immorality that sin has become accepted as everyday behavior. The naughty are often worshiped as heroes. The blame for criminal behavior is laid at the feet of society, or poverty, or discrimination. In lieu of the facts, the media now promotes a blatantly biased point of view and no longer has any compunction against censorship. Note Google,

YouTube, Facebook, and Twitter's July 2020 decision to remove the Capitol Hill Coronavirus press conference video from all their websites. In fact, the media seems bent on stripping America of her power and influence in the world.

Prosperity has spoiled us. We have borrowed recklessly, with little or no concern for the future, in order to maintain a lifestyle we cannot afford. We are proud. We have plenty. We love pleasure. We crave the mind-numbing filth turned out by Hollywood. The depths of our depravity are without limits.

In this new, declining country, the unborn cannot clamor for privilege, as members of special interest groups do. Instead, these helpless babies are now a burgeoning class of voteless and voiceless discards, victimized by the self-lovers who glory in their right to dictate life and death. We shamelessly murder millions of innocent babies, then employ foreign workers, mostly from our southern neighbors, to do our menial jobs because the bulk of our own citizenry is too lazy to commit to a day of physical labor.

Likewise, the sin of homosexuality is not only accepted but often lauded. Our government officials and politicians bow and cater to the homosexuals' open, boastful, and often militant demands for special rights, as if they are somehow an oppressed people. These people clamor for respect while they display rampant disrespect of and disdain for Christian and biblical values.

A Godless Land?

Has American turned her back on God? Certainly, most of our institutional infrastructures are godless. For this ethically-challenged generation, as God's Word has vanished from the public square, so too have our traditional Judeo-Christian values. The Word of God is publicly banned, and with it, we have lost our only true guide, for only God's Word can rightly govern the affairs of man. Nothing else is even remotely adequate. Only within God's Word can we find the unchangeable absolutes and laws that show us the way to salvation.

Lost, too, is God's invisible field of security around America. Much of the world hates us. Our enemies blackmail us with oil and threats of nuclear attacks. Others commit mass murder, flying our own planes into skyscrapers. Terrorist plots and homegrown cells put us under siege. Our borders are porous, hardly a barrier to crazed, impassioned enemies who long for our annihilation.

Should this great nation meet its demise, it would not be the first. The Persian Empire collapsed after only two centuries; Greece became mostly irrelevant after three. Even the mighty Roman Empire could maintain its powerful presence for only nine centuries. The citizens of these great entities probably imagined that their preeminence would last forever, but they were wrong. Exhibiting gross moral decline, they met their judgment at the hands of an outraged God.

In Os Guinness' *A Free People's Suicide*, he writes, "The plain fact is that no free and lasting civilization anywhere in history has so far been built on atheist foundations … A culture with no claims on its members—no curbs on their desires—would be a culture with no future. Freedom requires a firm refusal of what is false, what is bad, what is excessive, what is ugly, and above all, what a person is not and should never try to become. When everything is tolerable, nothing will be true; and when nothing is true, no one will be free."

Why, in such a short time, have basic Christian truths lost their influence over our once-godly nation? Why do we as a people bear so little resemblance to the brave souls who birthed us? Why has America been reduced to a second-rate nation, seemingly defenseless against a raging torrent of socialist insurgents, incurable diseases, and international terrorism?

We have lost our freedoms to a greedy government, bloated with "do-gooder" liberals acting as fronts for social redistributionists. These behind-the-scenes Marxists are determined to bring down the government that our forefathers fought so hard to build, and submit America to a state-run dictatorship where every citizen is rendered equally mediocre. ■

Chapter 2
Attack of the "Isms": Humanism, Liberalism, and Socialism

Old America … the glorious land of freedom and opportunity! How could she have fallen so far? Who is behind her demise?

We believe the dismantling of America and her foundational institutions is not by accident or default. Over the last nine decades, humanism, a "progressive" movement in which Man is the supreme being, has dumped its killer germs into the mainstream of American political, educational, economic, and religious thought. With that humanist movement has come the destruction of a country's history, its values, and its way of life. Humanism has wiped out nearly all that we as Christian traditionalists hold dear.

God Almighty has no role in humanism, which teaches that everything evolved into its present state by chance. In fact, humanists deny the existence of God altogether. Accordingly, they place man at the center of all things, the measure of all things. Man is his own god. He sets his own standards, his own definition of right and wrong. There are no divine absolutes to regulate his behavior. Humanists believe man is inherently good, and thus, he is in no need of salvation. He has no eternal soul. There was no Fall; consequently, there is no such thing as sin, no such place as Hell.

In the humanist world, man can love himself and find wholeness by being himself. Since man is the essence of reality, he is autonomous, self-sufficient, independent, and in full control of his own future. All he needs is education and training to actualize his human potential and intellectual awareness, and thus realize his most selfish fantasies.

Humanism has infected the very lifeblood of this once great country's existence. Its beliefs run rampant through an assortment of radical sub-movements such as liberalism, socialism, globalism, feminism, civil rights, gay rights, abortion rights, progressivism, communism, etc.

Ironically, if you look to the Bible, you can understand the doctrines of humanism just by replacing "God" with "Man." Every tenet of humanism is antithetical to the Word of God, just as Satan is the antithesis of God. If the Bible says yes, humanists say no. *The Humanist Manifesto* is the Devil's bible, and humanists are his disciples. Humanism and Christianity are direct opposites and cannot long coexist in the heart of man or in the nation in which he lives.

The phenomenal spread of this cancerous filth into every facet of American life can be attributed to massive, though sometimes nebulous, effort. Agencies like the American Humanist Association, the Aspen Institute for Humanistic Studies, the United Nations, and the ACLU are but the visible tip of the humanist iceberg. Through sophisticated networks, humanists have linked thousands of other organizations into

BIBLE (Word of God)	HUMANISM (Oracles of Satan)
There is one true God	There is no God
There is a Heaven and a Hell	There is no afterlife, no Heaven or Hell
There are eternal consequences of sin	There are no eternal consequences for sin
Homosexuality is a sin	Homosexuality is natural
Private ownership of property is good and right	Ownership of production and property belongs with the socialist state
God divided man at Tower of Babel by confusing their languages	Wants world community void of nationalism
God gave man dominion over the Earth and the animals, etc.	Man is to worship the Earth and promote animal rights
The Self is to be abased; Esteem others over self	The Self should be worshiped, promoted to god-like status
There are absolutes—values are fixed	The situation determines the action, values are fluid, no absolutes
Thou shalt not kill	Killing babies and old people is okay
Judaism and Christianity are distinct	There is good in all religions
God created all that is	All elements of the universe evolved
Man is born with a sinful nature	Man is inherently good
Liberty for all	All are slaves to the State

an invisible tapestry, camouflaged so as to be imperceptible to the naked eye. Then, with careful planning and dogged determination, they have planted members of these clubs in strategic policy-making positions throughout the country. In the twentieth century, as the humanist movement became more organized, it infiltrated every aspect of our society. Now the humanists control virtually all of America's corporate business developments, her education process, her press, her government, her entertainment business, and most of organized religion. As a result, humanism is legalized by her courts, legislated by her Congress, idolized by her schools, and sanctified by her churches.

While vestiges of Christian behavior still survive in the new America (and the majority of our citizens still claim to be Christians) humanists set the tone. Humanists are definitely the ones in charge of our country, regardless of who is in the White House. They control the preponderance of American behavior.

The mindless followers that comprise the humanist armies have no love for this country. They fashion themselves as citizens of the world. They love themselves and view God as a mythical crutch for the ignorant and weak of mind. They vote as they are programmed to. They are more tolerant of every religion in the world than they are of Christianity and Judaism. They shun and ridicule patriotic Americans with conservative values.

So broad-based is the New Age Movement, so engrained in all facets of our lives, that those who oppose it seem out of step. Humanism is the new norm. The mental composition of the American populace has been progressively and systematically altered, as the New American builds his or her everyday life around the humanist philosophy.

Humanism in Politics

Humanism manifests itself politically as liberalism and progressivism. For decades it has worked doggedly and, in the last few years, exponentially more effectively, to create a new America, with fully-converted New Americans. This invasive cancer has all but destroyed the Judeo-Christian infrastructure upon which this country was founded.

In his book *A Conservative History of the American Left*, Daniel J. Flynn writes about progressive reformers in America. "The state had to expand its size, reach, and control in the name of protecting the individual," Flynn writes. "Enlightened bureaucrats saw themselves as better equipped to spend people's money than the people themselves. They also believed it was the government's duty to redistribute resources and control prices and methods of manufacture." Thus, the leftist progressives sought to move away from the Constitution, which they believed to be outdated and inadequate.

An integral part of the liberals' second revolution is their silent "democratic revolution," in which a consortium of humanist factions have united and deceived enough of the ignorant masses to form a syndicated immoral majority. The majority then democratically elects leaders of the humanist persuasion who proceed to legislate anti-Christian dogma, as they slowly nudge America toward a one-world government, under global law. They proceed to confiscate and redistribute individual wealth (and, in many cases, individual means of earning a living) within America and to brazenly dispense our extorted monies to nations around the globe, to reduce disproportions in wealth worldwide. The "helping hand" extended to "underprivileged" groups is repaid as political clout.

Liberals and progressives in America toe the humanist line in their anti-American, anti-capitalist, anti-Christian positions, rulings, and laws. Owning practically all the media, they can cover for all the illegal acts of their comrades in government, even if he or she is the President of the United States.

As they take over our government, they enact laws and regulations that weaken our inherent structure. Through their rule, they will eventually cause us to be defeated by our many enemies, or forced to submit to global governance, with global economic control and international law. In the process, they defame America, bankrupt us, destroy our intelligence capabilities, and de-fund the military, leaving us virtually defenseless in an increasingly dangerous and nuclear-armed world.

Humanistic and Liberal Goals

Liberal socialists don't like the fact that God made some people smarter, more ambitious, more industrious, or more talented than He did others. So they bring in the government —a perfect weapon in the hands of the humanists—to take resources away from the productive in our society, through progressive taxation. They then redistribute these resources to the less productive, less capable, less motivated majority who has become their primary voting bloc. Thus they can stay in power ad infinitum.

Equality is the globalist's operational principle, his mantra, if you will. He pursues economic and social uniformity with religious fervor. He is determined to make the unequal equal, even if it means individual surrender and subordination to the state. Through the globalist liberal policies, Americans would once again submit to tyranny.

In the liberal vision, their reshaped, "ideal" American

would replace the "barbarians" and "deplorables" who support individual freedom and enterprise. America would now enjoy the "sophistication" of state collectivism. The new American would wed individual interests to those of the state. His social planners would mold society according to their will, with uniformity of thought and action.

Humanists vow to employ "whatever means are necessary" to bring about an end to wars. Hypocritically, they espouse violent protests and revolution as a means to end clan clashes and wars. Their true goal is to bring about a revolt against traditional values, patriotism, the taking of profits, and the accumulation of wealth, factors that they blame as the cause of wars, climate change, and disharmony among the races, cultures, and nation states.

To solve these alleged problems, the liberal revolution pushes with war-like fervor the following:

- Peace at any cost, even if it means the surrender of our freedoms
- Unity of all the world's races, cultures and peoples
- Globalism, socialism and communism
- Disarmament (personal and national)
- Establishment of a one-world government
- Redistribute wealth and resources (national and international)
- Abolish capitalism
- Establish a global community and economy
- Abolish biblical Christianity
- Anoint the State as our God
- Saving the Earth's climate from industrialized carbon-pumping capitalists

- Diversity as a camouflage for, of all things, oneness, all in an attempt to undo God's separation of peoples, races, and tongues at the Tower of Babel

If humanists mount a successful revolution, the end result will place Americans and all world citizens under an oppressive regime where freedoms are lost. The world will then be in the hands of a communist-like dictator, who could, in fact, be the Antichrist. Through universal digital surveillance and social management technology, this dictator could easily employ a tracking mechanism (maybe with a mark or a number) where he, and he alone, decides who lives and who dies.

Establishing a One-World Community

Beyond their stated objective of actualizing the self, humanists are driven by a compulsive desire to bring all nations together into a unified "world community." This transnational one-world conglomerate would, of course, be governed by international socialism, which liberals believe would abolish all nationalistic disputes, all destructive ideological distinctions, and all inflexible puritanical restraints. It would disarm the world powers. With this socialist government in place, the humanists envision a utopia in which men of all nations could peacefully coexist in a golden age of brotherhood and unequivocal unity.

As globalism takes hold, an oppressive regime of rules, regulations, and burdensome taxation will crush the great American-Christian foundation of liberty. We are not the only ones who see this appalling movement taking place in our country. In a *Chicago Tribune* column, March 15, 2016, Rosemary Warschawski wrote, "Conservatives feel their values and their way of life are under fire from a government that has stopped listening to them, that shuts them out of negotiations, that belittles their concerns, that is manipulating information to fortify a progressive agenda, and that is constricting free speech to stifle opposition ... Half of America is frightened that all that they have worked for, that the people they cherish, that the very structure and the rules by which they have organized their lives and for which they have paid a personal price are in danger.

"Liberals see the ship of state sailing to a Walden Pond-type body of water in which everyone will be content because everyone gets equal privileges, everyone is understood, and government and its systems will take care of them and keep the scary specter of responsibility at bay."

Disarmament

Property rights and gun ownership will also be victims in the new regime. Liberals want all citizens unarmed, so no one will have the means to resist the tyrannical liberal government that is coming. The liberals in power will demand full compliance from the populace, and strip them of all power to protest or resist.

Common sense tells us that "gun control" does nothing more than disarming law-abiding citizens, while leaving the criminal element of society armed and even more dangerous. Criminals will always find a way to acquire weapons. Take the city of Chicago as an example. The state of Illinois has one of the strictest sets of gun laws in the country (California is the strictest). Yet, in the first half of 2020, gun homicides in Chicago rose by 34% over 2019, and shootings rose by 42%, even though overall crime rates were down. Chicago's rate of gun homicides in 2016 was 25.1 per 100,000 residents, compared to 14.7 in Philadelphia and just 2.3 in New York. Chicago also "recovered" a high percentage of guns from its residents—243 per 100,000 residents. That's roughly on par with Philadelphia and much higher than Los Angeles or New York.

- Approximately 94% of public mass shootings since 1950 have occurred in "gun free zones"
- 80% of gun-related crimes are conducted with illegally-owned firearms
- In countries with more restrictive gun laws, mass killers also carry out their violent plans with such weapons as bombs, knives, or moving vehicles

Mr. Sean Hannity with *Fox News* wrote, "Every time there's a horrific mass shooting, especially in a public school, Democrat demagogues rush to the microphone and, blaming the weapons instead of the shooters, clamor for gun control. This attempt to emotionally manipulate people is extremely disingenuous."

Taking the concept of personal disarmament even further, liberals would like to see America itself militarily compromised, or downright defenseless. In the liberals' quest for globalism, America must fall from her place of prominence in the world. Her sovereignty must be sacrificed for "global" citizenship, her interest absorbed by the global regulatory architecture.

God's wall of protection around America is being torn down, brick by brick, by its own citizens. They willingly expose her to her enemies through unilateral disarmament, cuts in defense spending, and restrictions on the CIA. They allow America's enemies to own a threatening portion of our debt, our businesses, and our properties.

Abolishing Capitalism

In order for the liberal utopia to flourish, the free market model that transformed America into an economic powerhouse must be destroyed. Capitalism, the economic engine of America's past prosperity, is wounded and destined to die. Corporations and banks will be nationalized, life savings and retirement accounts wiped out, productive individuals and businesses saddled with the burden of supporting the socialistic reallocation of resources and wealth.

Humanists are not bashful about publicizing their disdain for the free market. *The Humanist Manifesto* states the liberal goal quite succinctly: "… a shared life in a shared world." Considering themselves intellectually superior, liberals insist that universal socialism, without the profit-driven vices of capitalism, can succeed in bringing about this fairytale world.

Liberals seek to abolish an individual's right to reap profits based on his effort and skill. *The Manifesto* states, "It is the moral obligation of the developed nations to provide … massive technical, agricultural, medical, and economic assistance … to the developing portions of the globe. World poverty must cease. Hence, extreme disproportions in wealth, income, and economic growth should be reduced on a worldwide basis." Humanists are firmly convinced that today's acquisitive and profit-motivated society is a failure, and that a radical change must be instituted, with everyone voluntarily and intelligently cooperating for the common good.

Has America's meteoric rise in prosperity necessitated its own demise? America is now associated with the terms "exploitation" and "colonialism." Liberals claim that America has grown rich at the expense of poorer nations. They seem delighted with the idea that abolishing capitalism would knock America off her high and mighty pedestal. And since the poorer nations are traditionally inhabited by people of color, successful white Americans have been made to feel guilty because they have food and material comfort, while the rest of the world starves.

In the liberals' new America, capitalism will be allowed to survive only so long as it can feed their massive redistribution of wealth. No matter how unfair, unjust, or damaging this policy is, the liberal would remove "disproportions in wealth," even if it kills the golden goose of capitalism in the process. The ignorant masses who buy into this liberal plot obey their masters, to keep the handouts coming. The handouts serve a two-fold purpose: to cripple capitalism and, more importantly, to buy enough support for humanists to put their master plan into play.

Do liberals hate our country and our market-driven system? At times their action certainly resembles hatred. But perhaps their fervor simply takes on the appearance of hatred as it drives them toward their goals. They must put aside any affections they may have had for the old America and her leaders in order to devise its downfall, for the sake of a "better world." Their hatred for former President Donald Trump is a prime example.

Abolishing Christianity

Obviously, the traditional economic system is not the only institution under siege by the liberals. In order to accomplish their takeover, they must also abolish traditional organized religion, especially Christianity. In its place, the liberal humanists would seek to establish a global religious structure. Humanists must synthesize all of man's divergent faiths into a comprehensive world religion, under the control of the global socialist government.

Quotes from *The Humanist Manifesto* illustrate why Christianity is a threat to humanist beliefs:

- "We begin with humans, not God. Nature, not deity."
- "False 'theologies of hope' and messianic ideologies, substituting new dogmas for old, cannot cope with existing world realities. They separate rather than unite peoples."
- "We can discover no divine purpose or providence for the human species."
- "The distinction between the sacred and the secular can no longer be maintained."
- "No deity will save us; we must save ourselves."

America was born a Christian nation and has always been a Christian nation, with God enshrined on her currency, her architecture, and in our hearts. The influences of Christian thought have been embedded in America's laws, customs, and holidays. Those who seek to destroy the old America know that a corrupted or collapsed Christianity would advance their process, for it is Biblical Christianity, its fundamental adherents, and its traditional value system that has contributed to America's uniqueness and greatness in the world. Christianity's operating principles have served as a bellwether for national behavior for nearly two hundred years. And during those years, we prospered, we were safe within our borders, and we were respected in the world.

Today, however, the humanists simply rewrite God's Word as they see fit: "We should reinterpret traditional religions and reinvest them with meanings appropriate to the current situation."

The reshaped humanist world structure would bring about the humanist's millennium. According to them, this millennium would be lauded for its spiritual experiences: experiences that transcend the sacred and merge the whole of human experience into a continuum of religious thought and activity. In its final stages, the movement would be like a religion.

H. G. Wells called the movement *The Open Conspiracy: Blue Prints for a World Revolution* and described it ultimately as more than just socialism or communism. He said, "It will be, frankly, a world religion" with a goal to "swallow up the entire population of the world and become the new human community." In search of their global utopia, humanists and socialists must marginalize Christians as exclusionary, high-minded bigots. In order to diminish the Christian impact on a changing world, traditional Christians must be mocked for their obsolete beliefs and behaviors. Eventually, they will be martyred to make way for the world's total acquiescence to the state religion of humanism.

Establishing the State as God

Proclaiming that God is dead and Christianity is a rotting corpse, the liberals are quick to offer up another god for us to worship—a benevolent god: the eternal state. The state guarantees that our needs will be met and our wants fulfilled. Since the state can put meaning in our life, why waste time worshipping a God that was probably no more than a figment of our imaginations in the first place?

In October 2019, US Attorney General William Barr summed up this worldwide trend in a speech at the University of Notre Dame, stating that the liberal, humanist movement threatens more than religious liberty in America. "First is the force, fervor, and comprehensiveness of the assault on religion we are experiencing today," Barr said. "This is not decay; it is organized destruction. Secularists, and their allies among the 'progressives,' have marshaled all the force of mass communications, popular culture, the entertainment industry, and academia in an unremitting assault on religion and traditional values. These instruments are used … to drown out and silence opposing voices, and to attack viciously and hold up to ridicule any dissenters. … The secular project has itself become a religion, pursued with religious fervor. It is taking on all the trappings of a religion, including inquisition and excommunication."

When liberals succeed in taking their socialist state to the point of godhood, their work will be done, their control complete. They're not quite there yet, but their progress is remarkable, and horrifying. They are preparing America for her role in the impending battle of Armageddon.

Sadly, new Americans don't care what happens to their country, so long as the checks keep coming. This new American apologizes incessantly for his country's "imperialistic behavior." He is openly enamored with the likes of Fidel Castro, Hugo Chavez, and Nicholas Maduro, in spite of the horrific economic and social strife in these socialists' countries. He supports the anti-American United Nations. He sends billions in foreign aid to countries and international money distributors that hate us. He allows millions of illegal aliens to live—*and vote*—in America.

The new American votes to regulate prices and profits. He votes for pork-barrel spending, for unread and hastily passed legislation, for robbing the "rich" and redistributing to the "under-privileged." The new American envisions a perfect world in which every citizen needs and accepts mothering by the state, cradle to grave.

Chicago Tribune columnist Rosemary Warschawski wrote, "If we continue leveling the playing field to the point of absurdity—where those who apply themselves and study according to the rules are passed over for those who have achieved much less; where people who work and sacrifice according to the rules are asked to give more of their money and the fruit of their labor to strangers who haven't worked; where people who have made what they consider to be moral choices are required to underwrite people whose choices offend them morally; and on and on—if we keep pushing that agenda, we are heading for a civil war or a revolution. Lacking the courage for either of these, America will become just another country, and the light of the world will grow dimmer." ■

Chapter 3
How the Liberals Seized Power

Over the last century, liberals have launched an all-out systematic war against the spiritual descendants of the very patriots who fought the British for our freedom in the 1700s. This second American Revolution has not been directed against a foreign foe, but it has instead been directed against her own citizens: their core beliefs and behaviors, their faith, their patriotism, their history, and their financial security.

These liberals are a dedicated family of groups banded together by humanist, socialist, and communist theory, determined to force not only the capitalists within America but throughout the world, to capitulate to socialism (which will eventually morph into totalitarian communism). Today, only a handful of nations have managed not to succumb. The U.S. is not officially socialist at this time, but she certainly has an ever-expanding socialist bent.

The liberal revolution aims to dismantle every vestige of Christianity, every aspect of the free market, every memory of who we really are and where we came from. To a large extent, liberals have won the culture wars and, in the process, trapped traditionalists inside an alien culture with only wispy remnants of our former glory swirling in nearly-forgotten corners of our minds.

For now, liberals attack not with guns and bombs, but with the silent killers of government, regulations, taxation, policies, and so-called reform. They march out an army of legislators, lawyers, judges, professors, social workers, journalists, union members, community organizers—and let's not forget the media—to overwhelm their foe. No segment of our society is untouched or untarnished by these foot soldiers. As they fight this war to further their own selfish and deluded agenda, they precipitate the undoing of all mankind.

The goal of the second revolution is universal socialism, absent any nationalistic allegiances. Liberals hope to use capitalism to finance their giveaway programs, and then dismantle and abolish private business. They would love to destroy every symbol, tradition, and biblically-sound doctrine of Christianity—along with anyone who believes in them.

The liberals have gradually but successfully fought this revolution, instilling their own ideologies without most Americans noticing. The majority of the populace does not realize that we live in a new America. Most cannot identify their true enemy. We have been pummeled with such an onslaught of radical changes to our faith and our traditions that we feel completely surrounded by the enemy, and we don't know who or what to fight. We don't even know where to begin.

Of course, many Americans are now sensing that something has gone very wrong, something is inexplicably different about our country. We see the apathy, self-absorption, and sense of entitlement that runs rampant through our society, along with growing violence. Yet, most of us feel utterly helpless to stop it.

The Dumbing-Down of America

The ignorant are more susceptible to propaganda, more easily led as sheep. Thus, liberals have set about "dumbing-down" America—its student body and work force—so as to make the citizenry more malleable. Through affirmative action (recently ruled unconstitutional by the Supreme Court), quotas, and reverse discrimination, liberals have forced schools and hiring managers to accept the less-qualified, while rejecting and demoralizing the qualified. Today, a diligent and intelligent White youth has far less chance of admission to the college of his choice than a neighbor from a minority group has, even if that non-White neighbor has significantly less-impressive credentials.

We used to think of Americans as the best and the brightest. But let's reexamine the facts. The Organization for Economic Co-operation and Development (OECD) released the results of the most recent global PISA rankings (Program for International Student Assessment, 2018) on student performance in mathematics, reading, and science. The U.S. did not even crack the Top 10. American students ranked 38th in Math, behind countries such as Poland, Italy, Russia, and even Vietnam. We were 14th in Reading and 19th in Science. China, by the way, was #1 in each of the three subjects.

As we dilute quality through reverse discrimination, we

also become less competitive in the global marketplace. The United States imports more than it exports, and it has a trade deficit of $49.4 billion as of mid-2020, with a deficit of $26 billion to China alone. Given our falling standards for success, who can be surprised by this decline in American productivity? Unable to accept the most promising college applicants, we have dumbed-down our education system to the point where we no longer produce enough high-level trained intellectuals to fill demanding positions in technology, medicine, research, etc. These jobs are now going to Asia and India, while the bulk of our manufacturing takes place in China.

The Blitz of Misinformation

Misinformation and outright lies are key weapons in the liberal war against traditional America. The Left feels so egotistically sure of their own righteousness that they have entitled themselves to create their own truth and concoct their own morality. There are no boundaries. They are "liars for justice."

For humanists, ethics are fluid—they can change them at will, depending on the needs of the situation. After all, they have no biblical set of absolutes to govern their lives. They can lie with impunity because they are accountable to no one. The media is in their back pocket and will never dispute them.

Psychological Warfare and Redirection

Liberals are masters of psychological warfare. Often their tactics are little more than child psychology used against a dumbed-down populace.

One of their common ploys is to project their transgressions onto the opposition. They falsely accuse conservatives of the very things they are guilty of. They also blame conservatives for all existing problems, and place scandalous labels on them. One of their favorite ploys is to claim that fascism will rise out of the political right. In fact, they equate patriotism with fascism.

Liberals excel at diverting blame or cushioning blows by saying they are simply mimicking the tactics of their opponents. Liberals are never wrong; conservatives are never right. In the rare occasion when they are caught in a lie or misdeed—rare indeed, since the media refuses to expose them—they respond with examples, often weak or irrelevant, of conservative misbehavior or faulty policy.

Yet, liberals blame conservatives for every failed or unpopular program or issue in our country. They never take responsibility for their own actions. They go so far as to claim victimhood while they victimize their foes. In the midst of hurling stones (literally, as seen in the riots after President Trump's election), they hide behind hollow claims of shameless mistreatment at the hands of the "vast right-wing conspiracy" or the Republican Attack Machine. The media clamors to agree with them.

Moral equivalence is another common liberal ploy as they try to equate minor Republican infractions with their own horrifying behavior. In 2017, we saw liberal comedian Kathy Griffin gleefully displaying President Trump's bloody dismembered head, and a liberal citizen opening fire on members of the Republican congressional baseball team on a practice field, hitting four people, including Steve Scalise, the majority whip of the House of Representatives. Riots broke out in cities across the U.S., following President Trump's election. And the justification? Trump's sexist remarks? The Republicans winning an election?

Trump has also been loudly criticized for his relationship with the Russian government, amid claims that Moscow tried to sway the presidential election in his favor. Intelligence officials concluded that persons connected to the Russian government leaked information about the Hillary Clinton campaign to WikiLeaks, so it could be released to undermine her. President Trump has repeatedly denied any collusion with Russia and described the allegations as a "witch hunt."

While everyone is screaming about Trump being in bed with Putin, only a few are brave enough to whisper of the connections between Russia and Hilary Clinton herself. In April of 2015, an article in the *New York Times* reported:

> **"Cash Flowed to Clinton Foundation Amid Russian Uranium Deal"**
>
> "… the Russian atomic energy agency, Rosatom, had taken over a Canadian company with uranium-mining stakes stretching from Central Asia to the American West. The deal made Rosatom one of the world's largest uranium producers and brought Mr. Putin closer to his goal of controlling much of the global uranium supply chain …
>
> "The leaders of the Canadian mining industry [who put the deal together] have been major donors to the

charitable endeavors of former President Bill Clinton and his family. Members of that group built, financed, and eventually sold off to the Russians a company that would become known as Uranium One. Beyond mines in Kazakhstan that are among the most lucrative in the world, the sale gave the Russians control of one-fifth of all uranium production capacity in the United States. Since uranium is considered a strategic asset, with implications for national security, the deal had to be approved by a committee composed of representatives from a number of United States government agencies. Among the agencies that eventually signed off was the State Department, then headed by Mr. Clinton's wife, Hillary Rodham Clinton.

"As the Russians gradually assumed control of Uranium One in three separate transactions from 2009 to 2013, Canadian records show, a flow of cash made its way to the Clinton Foundation. Uranium One's chairman used his family foundation to make four donations totaling $2.35 million. Those contributions were not publicly disclosed by the Clintons …

"And shortly after the Russians announced their intention to acquire a majority stake in Uranium One, Mr. Clinton received $500,000 for a Moscow speech from a Russian investment bank with links to the Kremlin that was promoting Uranium One stock."

Of course, Ms. Clinton would never stop at one or two infractions. In a November 2017 article, the *Wall Street Journal* describes, "one of the dirtiest tricks in U.S. political history":

> "The Democratic National Committee and the Clinton campaign hired the opposition-research firm Fusion GPS in April 2016 to dig up dirt on Donald Trump. Fusion in turn hired former U.K. spook Christopher Steele to assemble the (now largely discredited) dossier," (a dossier supposedly containing facts about Trump's wrongdoings)."

Ms. Clinton claimed that she did not release any details from the dossier until after the election, so that it wouldn't impact the election. As the *Wall Street Journal* reports, however:

> "This is utterly untrue. In British court documents Mr. Steele has acknowledged he briefed U.S. reporters about the dossier in September 2016. Those briefed included journalists from the *New York Times*, the *Washington Post*, *Yahoo News,* and others. Mr. Steele, by his own admission (in an interview with Mother Jones), also gave his dossier to the FBI in July 2016."

The article goes on to expose the truth about this dossier:

> "Among the dossier's contents were allegations that in early July 2016, Carter Page, sometimes described as a foreign-policy adviser to Candidate Trump, held a 'secret' meeting with two high-ranking Russians connected to President Vladimir Putin. It even claimed these Russians offered to give Mr. Page a 19% share in Russia's state oil company in return for a future President Trump lifting U.S. sanctions. This dossier allegation is ludicrous

on its face. Mr. Page was at most a minor figure in the campaign and has testified under oath that he never met the two men in question or had such a conversation.

"Yet, the press ran with it. On September 23, 2016, *Yahoo News*'s Michael Isikoff published a bombshell story under the headline: 'U.S. intel officials probe ties between Trump adviser and Kremlin.' Mr. Isikoff said 'U.S. officials' had 'received intelligence' about Mr. Page and Russians, and then went on to recite verbatim all the unfounded dossier allegations. He attributed all this to a 'well-placed Western intelligence source,' making it sound as if this info had come from someone in government rather than from an ex-spy-for-hire."

The liberal media is quick to accuse President Trump of alleged atrocities of all kinds, including collusion with Putin, but how much does the American public hear the true facts about the liberal leaders' own more significant and shocking misdeeds?

Demonizing the Enemy

Liberals play to win, and they play dirty. The poor soul who opposes the liberal agenda finds himself the target of venomous attacks on his beliefs. Everything is fair game in the liberals' war to win the heart and soul of our country, even if it means attacking an enemy's personal and family life.

To destroy the opposition and neutralize their positions, liberals invent derogatory catch-phrases and sinister-sounding labels, such as right-winger, homophobe, transphobe, religious right, sexist, racist, classist, statist, war-hawk, white supremacist, Nazi, Christianist, or fascist. These labels are assigned to anyone who disagrees with them, whether these people actually fit the labels or not. The robotic liberal corps of media propagandists carries on the charge, tattooing the false claims on the public brain with mind-numbing repetition. If you agree with them, the liberal media will let you get away with anything. However, if you disagree with them, they smear, slander, and even lie about you. They do whatever it takes to render you and your views meaningless in the public square.

Rather than debate the issues, liberals attack the messenger. They go for the person, not his positions; they kill his influence; they assassinate his character in the hope that his message will die along with his reputation. They marginalize him into silence. They berate and intimidate him, in smug, holier-than-thou tones, glaring down their noses as they portray him as a backward, Bible-thumping psych-ward lunatic. It is much easier for liberals to demonize the opposition than to argue against issues such as personal freedom, lower taxes, and less government. Liberals pin their opponents to the mat, leaving conservatives afraid to rise and speak out against the unfair and inaccurate accusations the liberals have heaped upon them, accusations such as "white privilege," which actually vanished years ago (and has been replaced, in fact, with Black privilege, as a result of all the biased government programs).

Obviously, demonization is working. It has cleverly maneuvered conservatives into a trap. If conservatives reject state intervention and entitlement programs (mostly designed for minorities), the liberals will label them as bigots. Hence, most conservatives give in and vote for government-run programs. Former President George W. Bush even touted his "compassionate conservatism" to garner favor with liberal constituents, but that gained him nothing, especially after the press got through with him. It only proved him a stoolie of the liberal establishment, while alienating true conservatives.

For the liberal, the agenda is all that matters (Stalin comes to mind, thrusting millions of dissidents into eternity so he could be free to execute his "plan"). For all their talk of standing up for individual rights, liberals actually consider individuals to be expendable, if they get in the way of the agenda.

As we draw closer to the end of time, we believe the Antichrist will take the liberal agenda one step farther, physically destroying all who oppose the progressive humanist plots. First on the annihilation list: Biblical Christians.

Creating a Whipping Boy

Anyone who reminds a liberal of the traditional, moral, patriotic America of yore is subject to ridicule, blame, and demonization. That goes double—no, triple—for the antithesis of the liberal movement: the conservative white male. Now the victim of extreme reverse discrimination, the white male has become the liberal whipping boy.

Think of the *Huffington Post* and other liberal responses to the capture of American Otto Warmbier, who was convicted for stealing a propaganda banner in North Korea and sentenced to 15 years' hard labor. The *Huffington Post* article, *"North Korea Proves Your White Male Privilege Is Not*

Universal," *Salon* called him "America's biggest idiot frat boy." The liberal press delighted in the tragic circumstances that would lead to Warmbier's death because he was a white male.

Liberals manufacture and peddle white guilt as a springboard to the passage of laws to redistribute the earnings of honest, hard-working citizens. They sport "identity" politics to promote the stature of their interest groups: feminists, blacks, Hispanics, homosexuals, etc. They stop at nothing to protect the unfair advantage that they seek to bestow upon the undeserving.

In this war on conservative white males, liberals have an ace in the hole—the race card. They are definitely not afraid to play it. If you are a conservative, you are automatically a racist. If you are against government-run healthcare, you are a racist. If you voted against Obama or opposed his policies, you are a racist. If you resist welfare programs for minorities, you are a racist.

We now see many whites succumbing to public pressure and buying into the guilt. They don't have racist beliefs or promote racist policies, but they're afraid of the label. They may even start to doubt themselves. They don't want to be associated with the outdated Bible-thumping rabble who, according to the liberals, make up 99% of the conservative party, so they side with liberals in their war against "angry white men." They believe this stance gives them the badge of sophistication, as part of the progressive, avant-garde society crowd.

Unfortunately, these would-be conservatives are now really nothing more than "useful idiots" to the vast left-wing conspiracy.

Creating Crises

A valuable weapon in the liberals' second revolution has been, and continues to be, the creation and exacerbation of crises, such as:

- Global warming
- Poverty
- Terrorism
- Racism and the shooting of innocent black men
- Corporate greed and corruption
- The housing collapse
- The health care crisis
- The COVID-19 pandemic
- War

In the manipulative hands of liberals, crises work wonders. They generate a heightened sense of emergency, making it easier for liberals to bypass conventional rules and legislate from the bottom of the deck. Screaming, "Crisis!" the liberals can short-circuit debate and deliberation, to bypass conventional rules. The fabricated sense of urgency releases the liberal from all constitutional constraints in his quest for absolute power. Crises help the liberals mobilize the masses, making them easier to manage and manipulate. The greater the crisis, the more freedom, privacy, and individualism people are willing to give up.

In a crisis situation, liberals can seize the opportunity to polarize society and expand government control over the economy, as well as other aspects of our lives. Blaming capitalism for the crisis simply facilitates their efforts to spread the wealth to their loyal constituents, while gaining more power for themselves.

It is natural for people to fear crisis. Fear is a strong motivator and has been used masterfully by liberal change agents to fashion a new America, as its citizens search frantically for solutions. Unfortunately, the liberals' so-called solutions have been mutating our existing issues into even bigger problems. Look at the world today. Are we any better off in the new America? Or have things gotten worse?

The PC Movement

Another amazingly effective weapon in the stealthy New American revolution is the insidious thought and speech control apparatus known as the Politically Correct (PC) movement. An indoctrination mechanism, the movement is designed to mold us all into uniformity of thought and action. Liberal warriors inflict a PC world on us by force, using both social pressure and legal regulations that, once again, successfully generate fear.

Because of the PC movement, people are now afraid to open their mouths, in case they might inadvertently say something that offends one of the protected minorities. Should they misspeak, they appear ignorant, backward, or worse yet, bigoted. The greatest fear of all is to be labeled a racist, Nazi, or fascist.

Isn't it the ultimate shameful irony that, in the "home of the brave," the land of free speech, we are actually afraid to talk openly anymore, for fear of cultural shaming? Especially harmful is the manner in which the "PC police" have silenced Christians from speaking their convictions against sin and sinful lifestyles, lest they be labeled prejudiced. We are not allowed to speak out against some of the influences we see ruining our country. Unfortunately, this PC movement has already taken a strong hold, and it is working.

The "PC Police" have, for all intents and purposes, paralyzed us. We are essentially locked within the walls of our own minds, where we think but dare not put words to those thoughts.

Squashing Free Speech

We have reached the terrifying time in history when any American who publicly expresses conservative views or support of a Republican President may have to fear retribution.

A July 2017 study by the Heterodox Academy shows that conservative students are afraid to express themselves due to backlash from both their peers and their professors. According to the study, right-leaning young adults fear that their political views could be criticized as "offensive." They also fear retaliation from professors in the form of lower grades, or punishment from their college administration for "thought-crime." Considering that most colleges have mechanisms to sanction wrong-thinkers, students have a valid concern.

And what conservative student wouldn't be concerned when they have college teachers tweeting statements such as those by Michael Isaacson, an economics professor at John Jay College in New York City: "The solution to American gun violence is more dead cops" (Twitter, December 2015), or "What's even the point of a cop that isn't dead?" (August 2017).

According to the National Association of Scholars, more than 90% of colleges "substantially restrict freedom of speech and association. In a statement released by the NAS and signed by over 440 professors, writers, scholars, and representatives of academic organizations, it says, "Higher education is the special place in society set aside for the freedom to seek the truth, but that freedom is under assault." Columbia University president Lee Bollinger tried to explain the phenomenon by saying that some speech was "offensive" and therefore "boundaries" on campus speech should be imposed.

A 2018 study conducted by the non-profit organization, More in Common, titled *Hidden Tribes: A Study of America's Polarized Landscape,* found that up to two-thirds of Americans feel there is "pressure to think a certain way" about sensitive issues such as immigration, race, and gender issues. Survey participants reported that they fear ridicule and harassment from their fellow citizens, which is often magnified by social media and can potentially lead to trouble at school or work. More than eighty percent of the study's participants felt that hate speech and political correctness are problems plaguing America today.

Eliminating Conservative Thought Through Violence

As a Woody Allen character observed in the 1979 film *Manhattan*, "A satirical piece in the *Times* is one thing, but bricks and baseball bats really get right to the point of it."

Violence compounds America's current free speech problem significantly.

In 2017, potential conservatives in Portland, OR; Berkeley, CA; Middlebury College in VT; and elsewhere, have faced violence or threats of violence from an organization calling themselves "Antifa." Although the group is ostensibly "anti-fascist," it has emerged as the militant fringe of #TheResistance against Donald Trump. Their victims may be anyone they believe could be a conservative or a Republican. Michael Isaacson, the professor quoted in the previous section, is active in the Antifa movement.

Acts of Antifa include:

- The annual Rose Festival parade in Portland, an annual event with a 110-year tradition, had to be cancelled in April of 2017, due to insufficient police resources to control the threatened violence. Members of Antifa had denounced the Republican Party of Multnomah County (which includes Portland), calling party members Nazis and Fascists, and warning, "Nazis will not march through Portland unopposed." In this group of "Nazis," they included marchers with "Trump flags" and "red MAGA hats" (MAGA = Make America Great Again). They warned that if Trump supporters marched, "We will have two hundred or more people rush into the parade … and drag and push those people out."
- In the days following Trump's election, masked protesters smashed store windows in Portland, and in early April, activists threw smoke bombs into a "Rally for Trump and

Freedom" in the Portland suburb of Vancouver, WA. A local paper said the ensuing melee resembled a mosh pit.

- Antifa agitators are thought to be responsible for much of the destruction in Washington, D.C., on Inauguration Day, 2017.
- In February of 2017, 150 black-clad, masked protesters violently disrupted UC Berkeley's plans to host a speech by Milo Yiannopoulos, a former Breitbart.com editor. These Antifa members or sympathizers broke store windows and hurled Molotov cocktails and rocks at police, causing $100,000 worth of damage.
- In March, protesters pushed and shoved conservative political scientist, Charles Murray, when he spoke at Middlebury College in Vermont.
- In April, a speaker named Heather MacDonald was physically blocked from the auditorium at Claremont McKenna College, where she was due to speak. A scholar at a right-of-center think-tank called the Manhattan Institute, Ms. MacDonald is a noted expert on the relationship between law enforcement and minorities. She was among the first to theorize that anti-police protests in Ferguson, Baltimore, Milwaukee, and elsewhere have facilitated an increase in urban crime.
- In June, liberal demonstrators and others associated with Antifa punched and threw eggs at people exiting a Trump rally in San Jose, California. An article in *It's Going Down* (an anarchist publication and website aligned with Antifa) celebrated the "righteous beatings."
- Antifa activists have also clashed with right-wing activists and police in cities including Philadelphia, Houston, and Hamburg, site of the 2017 G-20 Summit.

- In Philadelphia in September 2020, when Antifa members mistook one of their own protestors for a Trump supporter, they destroyed his car, with his dog inside.

Black Lives Matter Organization Joins the Disruptive Socialist Effort

During the protests occurring in May and June of 2020 under the banner of the Black Lives Matter organization, another Marxist-driven group, many demonstrations escalated into riots and looting. In Minneapolis, one of the buildings targeted and burnt to the ground by rioters was actually a six-story apartment building slated for low-income housing.

According to insurance claims filed as a result of the violent BLM protests throughout the country, by September 2020, the amount of insured damage due to arson, vandalism, and looting was estimated to reach $1-2 billion nationally, primarily in 20 major US cities. This figure does not cover the total damage caused by the rioting because riot-related damage is not commonly covered by insurance. The true overall tally of violence-related damage at the hands of BLM supporters may well exceed the $2 billion mark by a great deal.

Portland was also the scene of more than two straight months of violent Black Lives Matter protests following the May 25, 2020, death of black man George Floyd. In July 2020, black journalist Andrew Duncomb was stabbed by a known Antifa member named Blake Hampe. The attack with a seven-inch blade that barely missed Duncomb's spine was captured on video by a bystander. Duncomb believes he was targeted because of his conservative views. "They don't really care about Black lives," Dumcomb said, in an interview with *Fox News*. "They are using BLM as a front to carry out the senseless acts of assault against this country."

While both BLM's and Antifa's stated disapproval of white supremacists is laudable, there is very little evidence that they take action against actual fascists. They seem to be using the anti-fascism façade as an excuse to rail against Republicans and Trump supporters, or anyone with whom they disagree, politically or philosophically.

Antifa's Early Ties to Socialism

Antifa's roots date to the 1920s and '30s when militant leftists battled fascists in the streets of Germany, Italy, and Spain. President Trump's rise to power has rekindled Antifa activity in the United States, and now the group's tactics have elicited substantial support from the mainstream left.

Like Nazism, fascism is a leftist concept and a leftist movement. At their core, these philosophies represent ideologies of the centralized, all-powerful state. Fascism grew directly out of Marxism. Today, however, in typical liberal fashion, progressives try to redefine fascism as a phenomenon of the right. Since fascism and Nazism became associated with the Holocaust after World War II, progressives decided to cover up their leftist roots and simply scoot the term over from the left-hand column to the right. It can't be too surprising that they're trying to rewrite history, considering how they freely try to rewrite America's Constitution, and to dismiss the Word of God.

As observed in an article in *The Schwartz Report*, titled

"The Left Gone Violent" by Ian Tuttle, "… the main purpose of language—to describe reality—is replaced by the rival purpose of asserting power over it. … Using words to cloak reality makes it easier to dispose of that reality. Antifa are not satisfied with labeling people fascists; they want them to bleed on that account." Mr. Tuttle also points out that Antifa seems to believe that they alone have "the right to define who is a racist, fascist, or Nazi." Likewise, Ian Tuttle points out, these "… leftist thugs have appointed themselves adjudicators of the fates of … anyone they 'don't like,' and in this lawless realm, whatever crimes Antifa commits are not crimes, and their victims are not victims."

The 1970s in the U.S. were also marked by leftist violence, as chronicled in Bryan Burrough's book *Days of Rage: America's Radical Underground, the FBI, and the Forgotten Age of Revolutionary Violence*. This historic study covers the nearly daily occurrence of bombings by domestic underground groups, such as the Weathermen, the Symbionese Liberation Army, the FALN, and the Black Liberation Army—all groups dedicated to the violent overthrow of the American government. The bombings took place in locations such as urban skyscrapers, the Pentagon, the U.S. Capitol, a Boston courthouse, and a Wall Street restaurant packed with diners. One of the innocent citizens that died in these bombings was Frank Connor, a banker from New Jersey, killed by FALN's bomb at the historic Fraunces Tavern. Frank's son Joseph was quoted in *Burrough's Days of Rage*, saying, "They appointed themselves my father's judge, jury, and executioner. He represented something they didn't like, so they decided they had the right to kill him." Meanwhile, bombers such as Weather Underground members Bill Ayers and Bernadine Dohrn became celebrated academics because their violence had supposedly served the “correct” politics.

Just as the hatred exhibited by the Ku Klux Klan in decades past was deplorable, we should be equally shocked by the actions of the Antifa group, and others like it (Occupy, Black Lives Matter, the Black Panthers, etc.), as they demonstrate their own brand of hatred for anyone unlike them ideologically. Claiming “anticipatory self-defense,” they initiate violence and attacks on innocent citizens they have deemed “not us.”

A politicized fight culture is emerging. An editor at *It's Going Down*, said, “This sh@# is fun.” When violence is considered fun and conservatives are afraid to gather or speak for fear of being bludgeoned by masked thugs with batons, what's next? How can a house that is so savagely divided stand?

Our Losing Battle

For all intents and purposes, traditional Christian Americans have lost the culture wars. They have failed to recognize the enemy and his pernicious ways. Now, they are too weakened, spiritually, to defend traditional values against the white-hot fervor of liberal zealots. So relentless are these zealots that they have worn their opposition down. It now seems futile to resist, so most Christians have simply given up the fight.

With the culture wars won, the liberals can start dismantling civil society, piece by piece. They will continue in their quest to rid the country of all who maintain traditional values and institutions, all who stand as obstacles to their dream world.

The sad fact remains: the humanist/liberal revolution is succeeding. The liberal worldview has silently overwhelmed the Christian worldview. They've created a new America while systematically destroying the old. Biblical Christians and conservatives may launch a futile attempt to preserve the institutions and traditions with which this nation was founded, but face it: that America is gone. The age of innocence, kindness, and respect for others … that, too, is gone. ■

Chapter 4
Leftist Presidents Hasten America's Demise

Obama the Anointed

The meteoric rise to power of former President Barack Obama illustrates exactly how far the liberal machine has rolled in recent decades. Obama entered the political scene from out of nowhere and was wildly successful, heralded here and abroad as if he were The Answer the whole world had been waiting for. In a society where a rock star is the highest embodiment of celebrity, he was given "a rock star's welcome" wherever he went.

Traditional Americans, on the other hand, studied Obama's policies and trembled in fear. Surely, this person could not attain the position of the Leader of the Free World? We feared him, not because of the color of his skin, but because of his beliefs, his thinly-veiled plans for destroying our country. We thought—we prayed—that he could not be elected. We were wrong. It was as if he had been supernaturally empowered by "The Force": the powers of darkness and deception, the powers of Satan himself.

No matter what he might say to the contrary, as a doctrinaire Marxist, Obama shares the international left's disdain for America. Hiding behind his deceptive eloquence, he set about bankrupting America to further the causes of Marx and internationalism. His executive orders and hastily-passed legislation only accelerated the demise of America, bringing her, at best, to a position no better than on par with other countries.

Marx would indeed be proud of the way Obama nationalized vital American industries and pulled in his union buddies as partner-owners. Obama's army of foot soldiers and Czar coordinators fought the revolution in the trenches, while he directed every move from his white house. He fired "greedy" capitalist CEOs at will, with hardly a whimper of protest from the state-run propaganda machine. He knew he would march unchecked—for at least 8 years, thanks to the undying support from the ranks of ACORN, organized labor, peaceniks, feminists, civil rights groups, environmentalists, and especially the media.

Almost every informational and entertainment outlet in America covered for him, perpetuating his exalted position as their Anointed One. He was their mouthpiece, their hammer and sickle for radical change. The media elected Obama and kept him in power, regardless of how much damage he was doing to the country. They viewed his policies simply as the necessary pain that accompanies a metamorphosis into their global fairytale.

Liberal Media in Charge

Leading up to the election of 2020, the media took an even greater role than they did with Obama's election. Delighting in their ability to control the distribution of information, they went beyond covering for Biden, now bending or banishing the truth outright, through an appalling level of censorship. In the process, they launched an all-out war on Republican President Trump.

Consider this brief example, as cited in the *Washington Post* on July 7, 2020, summarizing CNN's coverage of President Trump's visit to Mt. Rushmore.

> "CNN called the massive carved sculptures of Lincoln, George Washington, Thomas Jefferson, and Teddy Roosevelt a 'monument of two slave owners' on 'land wrestled away from Native Americans.' When Obama visited the site, it was called 'majestic,' but somehow when President Trump was there, 'the site had morphed into a racist ode to slave owners.' "

In an example of downright censorship in July of 2020, Facebook, Twitter, and YouTube removed every online post of a White House press conference that spoke of progress made to tackle the COVID-19 crisis. Media outlets across the country slandered the doctors who had spoken at the press conference and cited "serious misinformation" as the reason to censor this news. Where were these champions of truth when false information about Trump's collusion with Russia spread like wildfire?

Beware the Antichrist

A cursory study of Obama shows us what to look for as we keep a vigilant eye out for the coming of the Antichrist. Obama embodies the qualities the Antichrist will possess: flaunting a lust for power, hatred for his enemies, deceitful eloquence, and the use of any means necessary to achieve his goals.

Obama firmly believed that he did indeed have all the answers, and that he will always be right. The problems in the country were someone else's fault. He held no national allegiance or certification of birth; the world was his stage, and it was his playground. His followers resembled cultists.

Obama masked his Antichrist spirit with a façade of faith. He claimed to be a Christian, while pushing an anti-Christian, Marxist agenda. Obama's mentors, associations, and advisors were Marxists. His tactics were radical (à la Saul Alinsky), and they were antithetical to those of Christ.

Above all, Obama was and still is a master deceiver, and a clever one at that. He has the ability to twist and torture the truth with a straight face. It staggers the mind of those who have the stomach to listen to him.

Examining Obama's Policies

Obama's presidency left us with a crippled country, which Donald Trump was trying to save and may have succeeded if he hadn't been fighting an uphill battle against hatred, prejudice, misunderstanding, and misinformation, perpetrated by a radically partial media. Now Joe Biden takes Obama's place, showing every sign of continuing the leftist policies that will ultimately bring about America's demise.

A brief review of the policies of Obama's eight years in office helps us understand the appalling trends of today's society, trends that Biden will continue and compound.

Israel – Obama sought to throw Israel on the chopping block by siding with her enemies. They offered the Muslims Israeli land in exchange for "peace." They forbade Israel to build new settlements on her own land and tried to strong-arm her to abandon her own defense. Meanwhile, Obama offered an olive branch to the Arab nations, with a fat check rolled around it.

The Economy – Obama campaigned for a "planned economy" as the surest way to achieve his redistributive ends. He sought to cripple capitalism in his Marxist quest for government-run business. He took unrestricted legal action against corporate America and leveraged his union buddies to stifle competition, slash productivity, and drive up costs for us all.

Redistribution – Obama relished his role as the divider-in-chief. He masterfully divided the "haves" and the "have-nots" to justify his attacks and taxations on prosperous capitalists. In essence, he believed the successful must be punished by paying for the failures or shortcomings of the less successful.

Housing – As a major player in the "Community Reinvestment Act," Obama contributed to the housing meltdown and subsequent financial crash of 2008 by forcing banks into sub-prime, uncollateralized, no-down-payment lending. After all, the collapse helped get him elected and paved the way for the gargantuan deficit spending he has inflicted on us and our descendants.

Legislation – Obama would have loved to write his own U.S. Constitution. He appointed two leftist judges to the Supreme Court, who decree by empathy and rewrite established law.

Environmentalism – Obama's so-called conservation efforts accomplished nothing but increasing energy costs. His caps on emissions and taxation of corporate offenders translated into higher costs for end-users. His "greening" policies are intent on greening the economy, not saving the planet. His environmental blackmail actually "reddens" our country, while squandering both our money and our freedoms.

Right to Life – Obama chose to kill babies, even after they are born, in the name of choice. He took this country to the extreme, to the point of no return. We are all at risk if our President can decide who lives and dies.

Disarmament – Obama sought to render us defenseless in a world that hates us, a world that stockpiles weapons to use against us. He advocated unilateral disarmament and nuclear arms reduction. He spoke endlessly of peace, while the world was poised to destroy us. Meanwhile, he proposed gun-control laws, to disarm us individually and render us powerless against criminals and a corrupt government. He wanted to face no resistance as he assumed total control.

The Left's Plans for Biden's Presidency

It's clear that Joe Biden, with the support of Democratic members of Congress and the Senate, plans to take Obama's socialist policies even farther. As outlined in Sean Hannity's study *Live Free or Die*, the intentions of the new liberal machine include:

- Abolishing private healthcare and socializing medicine through a Medicare-like program for all Americans
- Reversing Trump tax cuts and imposing a series of new taxes, including taxes on individuals as high as 70%
- Downsizing the military and other means of defending our country
- Abolishing the Second Amendment and banning all firearms
- Suppressing free speech
- Appointing leftist activist judges throughout our judicial system, including in the Supreme Court
- Promoting federally-funded abortion
- Establishing a guaranteed basic income, regardless of an individual's work status
- Expanding the welfare system and providing free services to illegal immigrants
- Opening our borders
- Ignoring Israel, in favor of more closely aligning with Arab nations
- Legalizing voting rights for convicted criminals
- Enacting laws that would reverse America's energy independence
- Empowering the government to micromanage the American people in most matters of their private and individual lives
- Supporting identity politics and evaluating people based on what they are, rather than who they are

Identity politics is at the heart of the Democratic Party today, as they fixate on race, gender, sexual orientation, and other groupings of humanity. It's ironic. As Owen Mason said in the *Washington Examiner*, "Isn't defining someone as what they are and not who they are the very opposite of liberal?"

President Biden is a blatant fan of this grouping concept. One of his campaign promises was to appoint the first black woman to the Supreme Court. As law professor Johnathan Turley pointed out in a tweet, Biden apparently wants to create "a race and gender prerequisite for appointments to the Court."

If Americans truly understood what Biden and his cronies were all about, he never would have been elected, in spite of Americans' general aversion to Donald Trump's personality. Unfortunately, most Americans are too lazy to probe deeply into a candidate or party's plans and too quick to believe the sound-bites of rhetoric they hear from the leftist media. They voted with their hearts, out of hatred for Trump, instead of voting with their intellect.

In fact, leading up to the 2020 election, anti-Trump sentiment became so vehement and extreme that many people were afraid to admit they were Trump supporters. The media, leftists leaders, and even their neighbors threw vicious barbs at Trump supporters, seeming to honestly believe that anyone who was a Republican could not also be a good person. In fact, they were deemed despicable people, or, as Hillary Clinton so eloquently put it, "deplorables." Antifa and BLM members branded Trump supporters as Nazis, and one FBI agent, Peter Strzok, decided that the only people voting for Trump were "smelly Walmart people." Obama himself once said this about right-wingers: "They get bitter, they cling to guns or religion or antipathy to people who aren't like them, or anti-immigrant sentiment or anti-trade sentiment as a way to explain their frustrations," (as quoted in an April 14, 2008, article in *The Guardian*).

Trump's Legacy

Clearly the Democrats want no obstacle to their plans or their power. They will do everything within their power to discredit everything that Trump did. Was Trump, however, a bad President? Certainly he realized what the liberals had done to the country, and was trying to "make America great again." In our opinion, and that of many other scholars, he was on the right track in many ways, although most Americans have no concept of all that he accomplished.

From his book *Live Free or Die*, Sean Hannity highlighted the numerous accomplishments of Donald Trump in his four years in office. Here are a few:

- Record-setting tax cuts
- Lucrative trade deals
- Greater energy independence
- Revival in domestic manufacturing
- Opportunity Zones that spurred investment and job creation in forgotten communities
- Regulatory reforms
- Greater national security
- The best employment numbers in fifty years
- A significant reduction in poverty

- Social Security protection for seniors
- A renewed sense of patriotism
- A sensible reaction to the COVID-19 virus that did not completely derail the American economy

While Obama sought to weaken the United States' relationship with Israel, President Trump did much to heal the connection between the countries. In 2018, he fulfilled his promise to recognize Jerusalem as the capital of Israel by moving the U.S. Embassy there. Trump also withdrew the U.S. from UNESCO, due to the organization's anti-Israel bias. In 2019, Trump formally recognized Israeli sovereignty over the Golan Heights, while re-imposing sanctions on Iran. Israeli president Netanyahu told President Trump, "Israel has never had a better friend than you."

President Trump also energetically defended religious liberty in America. At the 2019 Values Voter Summit, Trump said, "On every front, the ultra-left is raging war on the values shared by everyone in this room. They are trying to silence and punish the speech of Christians and religious believers of all faiths. … They are trying to use the courts to rewrite the laws, undermine democracy, and force through an agenda they can't pass at the ballot box. They are trying to hound you from the workplace, expel you from the public square, weaken the American family, and indoctrinate our children. They resent and disdain faithful Americans who hold fast to our nation's historic values. … We know that families and churches, not government officials, know best how to create strong and loving communities. … And above all else, we know this: in America, we don't worship government, we worship God."

With his America First policies, Donald Trump stood in the way of corporate America's plans to continue expanding their profits through globalism. In many cases, he was the only thing stopping the globalist elites from sacrificing our homeland in exchange for money in their pockets.

Trump did his best to hinder the liberal, anti-American assault on our values and traditions, but with Biden in office, his positive affect has been short-lived. ■

Chapter 5
The Dark Side of Democracy

America was founded as a Republic but built upon a system that failed to stress a nation under the divine jurisdiction of God. Consequently, the nation has, in the name of religious pluralism, abandoned its safe haven "under God" and rejected the vision the American Pilgrim and Puritan founders had for their new home. With the loss of traditional Judeo-Christian values like humility and love for others, democracy can, in fact, become an utter failure.

As our republic grew less righteous, it also became more democratic, reaching today's point of almost pure democracy, where everyone votes, regardless of their stake in our nation's survival. The humanists' democracy exalts the individual self, giving even the most ignorant and least contributory voters a voice in the allocation of our nation's wealth and the legislation of immorality. As such, uneducated, uncaring voters assume godlike status.

If 51% of the nation votes to legalize immorality, then it is right in the eyes of the law. That goes for abortion, homosexual marriages, etc. God says these acts are sins, but when the majority makes them the law of the land, then the voice of the people, by default, becomes the voice of God. The dark side of democracy is exposed, as the will of God is supplanted by the will of an immoral majority. The citizenry can disregard God's decrees on sin, and invent their own definition of right and wrong.

Liberals love democracy because of the ease with which they are able to steal elections. At election time, they have brigades of foot soldiers from ACORN, the unions, the NEA, etc., at their disposal, to register throngs of potential voters (alive, dead—doesn't matter) to overwhelm the system. They bus their followers to the polls as part of their "get out the vote" program. Other liberal tricks include bribery, intimidation, demonizing the opposition, pushing class jealousy and prejudices, doling out dollars, motor voter campaigns, and inciting racial and ethnic divisions (probably the most fraud-ridden process of the lot).

Of course, liberals don't believe in sin and the biblical view of right and wrong. They don't care if they trample on God's Word en route to remaking our Christian America into a humanist stronghold. In a pure democracy, there is nothing to check the majority from ganging up on the minority, sacrificing the weaker party to the omnipotence of numbers, the totalitarian poison of popular rule. Simply put, democracy is a lethal weapon in the wrong hands.

In leftist democracies, we see liberals abuse the honorable intentions of government processes to accomplish their own purposes, exploiting the system to:

- Supplant the will of God with the will of man
- Rewrite the Constitution
- Secure one-party rule
- Tax their opposition while denying them representation
- Redistribute the wealth
- Enslave capitalism and enthrone socialism
- Usher in a dictatorship

The liberals' version of corrupted democracy is sickening to anyone who cherishes justice.

From Democracy to Dictatorship

The sad truth about universal suffrage is that it leads to one-party rule and, ultimately, the end of democracy. Democracy self-destructs when morals collapse and self-lovers vote themselves generous gifts from the public treasury. The well runs dry, chaos ensues, and a dictator arises to restore order. In the process, of course, freedom is lost.

Progressive lowering of voting standards has been integral to the democratization of our Republic, and subsequent collapse into mob-induced socialism. In fact, liberals have corrupted the democratic process so much that now dead people vote and live people vote more than once. Even Mickey Mouse has a say in who goes to D.C.

Democracy is, in fact, a temporary form of government on the way to a totalitarian regime. What a wonderful tool democracy has proven to be for liberals to peaceably hijack our government, ultimately paving the way for the Antichrist, on a global scale. ■

Chapter 6
Socialism vs. Capitalism

Though hobbled by an array of taxes, rules and regulations, corporate business magnates today still wield unprecedented power as they command global respect. They grow rich because they have, for now, the freedom, flexibility, and opportunity to employ their skills and their resources to grow their wealth.

The reward for their efforts comes in the form of profits. Are profits despicable, as liberals so contentiously argue? Would the world population truly be better off under a socialist, state-owned and state-managed economy?

The History and Philosophy of Capitalism

Though hardly the complex system we have today, the use of commerce to expand markets and accumulate wealth has existed for thousands of years. An ancient form of capitalism began in Egypt and spread to Mesopotamia and, eventually, the other five world empires. However, with the demise of the Roman Empire in A.D. 476, free enterprise subsided and world trade declined. Through the ensuing Dark Ages, and for the next thousand years, the standard of living plummeted as capitalism gave way to feudalism.

During medieval days, people believed that life was just a test, determining whether the soul would be saved or damned after death. The Renaissance and the Protestant Reformation brought a revolution of new ideas that were to influence capitalistic principles for generations to come. During the Renaissance, humanist thought prevailed, and life was considered an end in itself. Contrary to Biblical precepts, this humanist outlook stressed the desirability of material advancement and improved living conditions.

The medieval feudal system, with its nobility, strict social class system, and hereditary landlords, was destined to die. Its death was precipitated in part by the resurrection of private enterprise. The Christian Crusades and the discovery of America helped trigger capitalism's revival, after hundreds of years of dormancy. The Crusades initiated renewed international trade, and Columbus' 1492 voyage introduced new trade routes, as well as a staggering wealth of New World resources to Western Europe. Those riches would later be used to help finance the Industrial Revolution, during which a massive input of capital produced extraordinary outputs of merchandise. Production for personal use gave way to production for sale. Modern capitalism was born.

Until the 18th century, most industrial production took place in small, privately-owned workshops. The Industrial Revolution brought the concentration of production into the hands of wealthy capitalists and independent factory owners.

At the same time, powerful landlords were driving small farmers out of business and into town, where they became a source of cheap and abundant labor. With heavy investments in equipment and human resources, capitalists created a profit-producing marriage of man and machine.

Meanwhile, the Protestant Reformation, founded upon predominantly sound doctrine, also introduced several ideas that complemented the humanism of the Renaissance. Most notable were the teachings of John Calvin. He "legalized" the collection of interest on loaned money and encouraged savings. He also stimulated a materialistic drive among Protestants, by interpreting "predestination" in such a way that made business success appear to be a mark of God's favor.

By Calvin's standards, God blessed 18th and 19th century capitalists. Owners of businesses often grew rich, and those who sold their labor to growing companies also prospered. The standard of living in industrialized countries improved. The world's insatiable appetite for new capital also brought prosperity to financial institutions and investment bankers with international affiliations.

During these early years of modern capitalism, governments adopted a "hands off," laissez-faire policy. Independent, unsubsidized firms operated in an environment of unobstructed competition – competition designed to bring success to the most efficient producers. Governments at that time felt that was the way it should be. Corporations evolved and continued to grow as the beginning of the 20th century ushered in a period of peace and prosperity.

In October 1929, the bubble burst. The stock market

crashed and the Great Depression that followed dropped capitalism to its knees. When it struggled back to its feet after eleven years of despair, private enterprise was forever altered. Enterprise was now tasked with alleviating the misery of its "victims." Capitalism was saddled with the responsibility of securing both the present and prospective needs of every member of society, whether they contributed to the economic structure or not. Social (state-managed) capitalism evolved and swept over the world of heretofore-free economies.

Following the Great Depression and the ensuing social reforms, capitalism in the late 20th century enjoyed unprecedented wealth, sharing (perhaps involuntarily) its blessings with more people than ever before. In spite of profit-robbing legislation and taxation, capitalism ironically became even more profitable in the second half of the 20th century.

We can attribute much of capitalism's success to greater managerial efficiency, ingenuity, and aggressiveness. Giant corporations were now managed by highly-trained professionals rather than individul owners. Process automation resulted in significantly higher levels of productivity. Rapid advances in computer-based technology offered even greater potential for mechanization of manual efforts. Aggressive financial services, here and abroad, generated fortunes in interest dollars for capital-rich investment firms. Increased wages, benefits, and welfare packages aided business by pumping billions of dollars back into a capitalist economy. Consumers had more money, and, as is the case with most Americans, they spent it. The law of supply and demand drove prices up and businesses prospered.

Prices climbed after trade unions extracted increased wage and benefit packages from reluctant profit-conscious corporations. The never-ending spiral of increased costs followed by higher prices generally favored the corporation. In essence, capitalism shared enough of its bounty with the working class to buy them off, while it rebounded from near collapse into the most prosperous haven of private enterprise in history.

Unfortunately, in periods of great prosperity, morality declines. By the mid-20th century, Americans started tossing their traditional values aside. Then the liberals took over, driving the country toward financial ruin.

Trillions of dollars in debt, we can no longer boast of American prosperity. Recent economic crises are accelerating the demise of capitalism at the hands of its archenemy: socialism.

The Abuse of Capitalism

Clearly, socialists hate capitalism, while liberals tolerate it, as long as they can redistribute the resulting wealth to stay in power. The only opinion that should really matter to us, however, is God's. Does God favor capitalism? Or is there something about the spirit, attitude, or driving force within the system that is repulsive to Him?

God, of the Christian Bible, has always advocated man's economic freedom and individual responsibility. That freedom and responsibility must include rights such as owning property, excelling in a vocation of his choice, providing goods and services, supporting his family, helping the needy, and putting enough aside for a rainy day. In other words, the Bible suggests that God supports the concepts of free enterprise and pure capitalism. This author does too, emphatically.

Man's economic freedom comes in the form of profits. There is nothing wrong with that. Nothing wrong with man's natural desire to improve himself, or to reap the rewards of his talent, energy, and skills. Nothing wrong with gain that comes from the exercise of a man's invention, self-sacrifice, and enterprising nature. Taking a profit is purely in keeping with God's plan for man, as long as the profit is acquired honestly and no one is hurt in the process.

Thus, the concept behind private enterprise is not inherently evil. Within the capitalist drive for profit, however, there can indeed be elements that defy God's laws. In the eyes of God, there is a difference between pure capitalism and corrupt capitalism.

Abuses of privilege and misuse of capitalism's freedoms separate good, old-fashioned private ownership from the impure manipulation of capitalism. As soon as these abuses enter an individually- or corporately-owned business, God's sanction departs. These economic affairs then slither under the unloving administration of an unholy spirit.

With the willful perversion of the freedoms of capitalism, man can mutate free enterprise into a competitive, ever-expanding monster, devoid of human compassion. In this deviant form of capitalism, man merges equipment and human labor into a profit-producing machine that is incapable of looking beyond its own voracious appetite for higher and higher profits.

This form of corrupt capitalism lends itself to man's

natural desire for fun, fame, and fortune. Pursuing an unholy love of profit, man turns his focus to selfish desires, seeking gratification through material things, forsaking the rights of others, and perverting the love of God into a maddened craze for pleasure, possessions, and prestige.

Certainly, not all privately-owned enterprises are holy in nature, nor do all corporations harbor the spirit of greed and ill-gotten gain. By the same token, any business, regardless of its size, can be possessed by an unholy spirit. Pride, covetousness, and the pursuit of pleasure can motivate even the smallest businessman, making him, like his corporate counterparts, yet another cog in the humanist's wheel of self-fulfillment.

A business driven by this unholy spirit is not content to merely cover costs and make a reasonable profit. It exists solely to make more. Accordingly, its every act is directed at higher numbers on the bottom line of the financial report. Any technique that enhances the profit graph will gain management approval. Both the employee and the consumer are regarded as mere pawns in the system. Their value is measured only in terms of their contribution to the business.

When the bottom line looms as the driving force behind nearly every management decision, those decisions eventually and inevitably lead to expansion. Thus, the corrupt version of capitalism has no limits. It is relentlessly driven by greed to innovate and increase output. To increase profits, companies lower production costs. This, in turn, requires increased scales of production, resulting in centralization. Mergers, acquisitions, and takeovers concentrate most corporate wealth and power into the hands of only a few major corporations.

This dangerous concentration takes a deadly toll on the small businessman, but the loss of human compassion and understanding is far more devastating. Capitalistic expansion stomps on our basic human need to feel wanted and loved.

Today, humanism's corrupt version of capitalism has lost God's favor, as it outgrows the "old-fashioned" ideas of fair pricing, concern for others, and consideration for those who build and buy its products. With the growth of humanistic capitalism, compassion has steadily been replaced by greed, and love has given way to selfishness. These traits are far from the Christian ideal.

The Haves and Have-Nots

With advantage must come, of necessity, disadvantage. Invariably the weak suffer most in a fully competitive environment. The corrupt businessman adopts Darwin's "survival of the fittest" philosophy, and throws himself with religious fervor into the competitive struggle for superiority within the corporate structure. He has little compassion for losers but is exceedingly proud of his position as an affluent winner.

This type of capitalist contends that capitalism did not cause poverty; it only made poverty more visible by drawing the poor away from the farm and into the urban centers of manufacturing and commerce. In the pre-industrialized society, almost everyone was a farmer, barely surviving on their small plots of land. The majority of the population existed in the same financial fix. Therefore, poverty was less noticeable because most people were poor, at least by today's standard. With the prosperity of commercial growth, industrialists and workers both rose to affluence, thereby driving a wedge between those inside and outside the capitalistic structure. Those on the inside were the ones with the power to call the shots.

An increasing price structure perpetuates the economic distinction between the upper classes, middle classes, and the poor. As product prices continue to rise, those inside the economic order tend to maintain or improve their status, while those on the outside get poorer.

We see it happening all over the world. Sixty percent of the world's population has an income at or below the level of bare subsistence. A century ago, per capita income in developed nations averaged two times more than income in less developed countries. Today, the difference has grown to five times as much. The disparity widens. Capitalism has created a world after its own image, and those who do not join the competition will not survive.

Socialists in government force capitalists to share much of their bounty with the less fortunate. The increased costs of welfare are followed by higher prices and inflation, which only serves to shift everyone proportionately upward. The poor remain at the bottom of the socioeconomic ladder, worse off than before because they have no one to whom they can pass along price increases. As long as the competitive system survives in its unholy marriage with socialism (complete with government handouts and foreign aid) the poor will stay poor, and some of the rich will get richer, especially if they have liberal friends in the right places.

God cannot condone this type of capitalism. The system will fail, but not because everyone in America suddenly adopts Christian values and applies them to their business life. Sadly, most Americans, including Christians, are determined to preserve or improve their current lifestyles and the economic system that secures it. The downward spiral will continue, creating an ever-more-dismal state of affairs, and bringing about its own demise in the Great Tribulation.

The History and Philosophy of Socialism

Concurrent with and contributing to the dramatic change in capitalism was the spread of socialism, which took many forms, the most coercive of which was Communism.

Nineteenth-century German economist Karl Marx was primarily responsible for the man-centered philosophies of both socialism and communism. His writings gained popularity after his death and then exploded, as the most catastrophic phenomenon of the 20th century.

Marx's ideas clashed with the predominant capitalistic order. Under Marxist "democratic revolutions," the working class leveraged their numerical superiority to wrest political control from capitalists, thereby transforming the state into socialism. Socialist states could still enjoy some political freedom and some civil liberties, but without the economic individualism present under capitalism. In theory, the state would offer security and economic equality to all, regardless of their job status. Ideally, the state-supported system would evolve upward until the nation experienced utopian bliss. The utopian benefits would be available to everyone, all without any help whatsoever from the Christian God.

Marx did not believe there was a God that man could trust, or to whom he should be subservient. He was convinced that God was simply a projection of man's ideals, created by unfulfilled human desires for humane, just, and loving relationships. In other words, God was all in your head. Therefore, Marx had no argument with a preeminent state or a deified man.

Marx also believed that man does not act as a free agent, but responds only to external stimuli. In other words, man is a product of his environment, particularly his economic environment. In his teachings, the evils of the world are not the result of man's sinful nature, but are in fact products of institutions. The primary institution of evil, to Marx and his successors, was private enterprise, as it exists under capitalism. Remove those capitalist institutions, and you get happiness, right? So, Marx set about creating conditions in which human desires could be fulfilled and evils eradicated.

Paradoxically, Marx also viewed capitalism as necessary in the evolutionary process. He appreciated the production capabilities of private enterprise, and wanted to use those capabilities to fund the transformation of the state into socialism, with wealth for all. Thus, the products of capitalism could be turned into vehicles of social reform, financing socialistic human development projects and allowing man the leisure to develop his own creative potential.

However, the benefits derived from capitalism could not be fully realized as long as production and distribution capabilities were privately owned. Marx argued that workers never received wages that were equivalent to the value of the commodity they produced, because the capitalist business owners wanted to keep profits to themselves. Meanwhile, he claimed, those greedy owners tried to increase profits by driving workers to greater levels of productivity. Since Marx felt that business owners were basically stealing profits from their employees, he sought to unite the workers of the world to rise up against the capitalist system.

Ultimately, Marx wanted to remove the profit motive altogether, thinking that the inherent evils within capitalism would then disappear. He wanted to end private ownership of business and replace it with public ownership. Of course, "public" should be translated as "government" because, in socialism, the state eventually assumes ownership or control of all institutions.

Under the Radar

In an article titled "The Fruits of Socialism" by Charles Scaliger, the author states that socialism can "appear to be benign because post-Cold War socialism is not yet as totalitarian as the Stalinist regimes of the former Eastern Bloc and Mao's Communist China... modern socialist countries have not reached the extreme circumstances of Cambodia under the Khmer Rouge, Germany under the Nazis, or the former Soviet Union..." Thus, for "Western countries with vast amounts of wealth accrued from previous generations of free market capitalism, socialism appears, for the time being, to be an affordable conceit."

It appears that right now, socialism can creep in under our radar. Mr. Scaliger, who has lived in socialist countries for years, closely studying their politics and economics, as well as forming close relationships with their citizens, goes on to say, "Because most such countries have not erected Iron Curtain-style borders to isolate them from the free world, nor possess fearsome arsenals of weapons of mass destruction, their plight, unlike the former Eastern Bloc countries, passes largely unnoticed in the West."

Unwilling Bedfellows

Under Marxism, countries ruled by authoritarian monarchs or dictators experienced brutal communist-style revolutions. In democracies, socialists pressed for revolutionary changes through education, legislation, and trade union negotiation, so the change took longer and was more subtle. Many Western European countries are a showcase for Marx's state-controlled economies. Following years of infiltration, Europe is now principally dominated by socialist policies and governments.

Although Europe has fallen, America has not yet experienced a total conversion to socialism, even after decades of relentless socialist attacks. However, she has adopted, through the democratic process, so many of Marx's theories that countless demands have been placed on her once-free economic process.

With great success, socialists have legislated their archrival into a rather effective ally. Marxist-inspired leaders, such as Obama, have greatly accelerated the process. Along with legislation has come taxation. By taxing producers and donating the proceeds to non-producers, the state redistributes huge chunks of this country's corporate (and personal) wealth. In just five decades, the government's war on poverty has cost American taxpayers trillions.

Honest Americans are saddened and sickened by the exorbitant cost of their government's social programs. Even more disheartening is the political ineptitude and reluctance of elected officials to make changes, even though studies show their pet projects to be wasteful, ineffective, or destined for bankruptcy.

An example of misguided government intervention is the minimum wage law. Intended to help low-paid workers with less marketable skills, these laws actually have the opposite result, harming the people they intended to help, along with everyone else in the country. Employers can only cover the business costs of increased wages by responding with higher prices, and thus making it harder for everyone, especially the unskilled workers, to make ends meet. Business owners may also react to mandatory wage hikes by firing or refusing to hire workers in the minimum wage category.

Massive tax transfers to the poor in the form of food stamps, free medical care, and housing supplements are also examples of misguided government interference. Welfare in the U.S. is woefully counterproductive, as it strips the U.S. worker of motivation and incentive. Why work if you can make as much or more than your employed neighbors by simply staying home and watching TV? If you're a single mother, why get married, if the government will pay you to remain unmarried? It will also pay for your illegitimate babies, so don't worry about unplanned pregnancies. In fact, welfare has decreased the quality of life for America's lower class because of the disabling, binding, and perpetuating character of the government handouts.

The Reality of Socialism

Some may try to assert that the world's impoverished countries owe their problems to corruption rather than socialism. However, history has proven that corruption is in fact a by-product of socialism. Consider East Germany's communist dictator Erich Honecker, who was at one time believed to be pure in both ideology and lifestyle. With the removal of the Berlin Wall, the world learned the truth. Not only had Honecker personally ordered escapees from the Iron Curtain to be shot on sight, but he had, along with all his ministers, lived a life of greed and corruption. As reported in the *New York Times* in 1989, the exploits of the East German leaders included multiple lavish estates, confiscating land from villages in order to create private hunting lodges, and peddling arms, antiques, and luxury household goods from the West. As the *Frankfurter Allgemeine* wrote, the German Democratic Republic was "just another banana republic."

Through Charles Scaliger's broad experiences in socialist countries, he is qualified to bring us great insight about the reality of today's socialism:

- No competition. "Manufacturers (including, of course, state-run concerns) have little incentive to monitor or improve the quality of their products," which therefore perform poorly and break easily. These states have access to the same technology we do, but don't make good use of it.
- No freedom of choice.

- "Most consumer products are manufactured by state-run monopolies, which produce one brand, of middling quality at best."
- "Because socialists are certain of the adequacy of socialism to provide necessary goods and services, would-be foreign competitors are rigorously excluded from local markets."
- No respect for the law. "The law is used as an instrument for plunder," and thus is chiefly ignored.
- Poor infrastructure. Public provisions such as electrical grids, highways and bridges are totally inadequate. Mr. Scaliger reports that in the socialist country in which he currently lives (as of August 2017), electrical black-outs are a near-daily occurrence.
- Redistribution of wealth, but not from the rich to the poor. Instead, socialist countries "redistribute wealth from private citizens to the government and certain select cronies."
- Dishonesty and corruption. According to Mr. Scaliger, "Government officials … are almost all corrupt … unwilling to discharge any of their official duties without a bribe."

Mr. Scaliger says, "All of this is part and parcel of the social and moral order, or lack thereof, encouraged by the irrational and immoral structure of socialist government … The cynical exploitation of one's fellow man is necessary and morally justifiable."

Violence is also the reality of socialism. As Robert B. Charles wrote in his article, *The Battle of Big Ideas*, "Socialism is at heart a political and economic philosophy that holds that government … should use all means—including violence—to control property, production, distribution, and all civil activities."

Later in the article, Mr. Charles continued, "When party elites take over private property, national production, distribution, jobs, benefits, and where earned money goes, the end is approaching. Greater suppression follows, ends justifying means, until killing becomes part of how a society gets to utopia."

Sean Hannity agrees, in his book, *Live Free or Die*. He said, "Socialists these days cite 'social justice' as their goal, but socialism is not focused on achieving justice of any kind. Instead, its main impulses are rage, envy, scapegoating, a thirst for vengeance, and a desire to violently overturn the entire existing order." Mr. Hannity sees the history of socialism as a plan for creating an entire class of scapegoats, guilty of causing everyone else's misery, and a declaration of "open season" on those people. Socialism promises utopia, as long as you can bring about the annihilation of all class enemies. Mr. Hannity said, "Once you understand this, you understand why socialism so often degenerates into mass murder."

The goal of socialist groups such as Antifa and Black Lives Matter is to overthrow the government. As Mr. Charles said, "There is no halfway point. Their aim is power and bending society to socialist control."

Socialism Disguised as Environmentalism

In *Live Free or Die*, Sean Hannity clearly takes a hard look at socialism, voicing the same fears that we have regarding the current trends in America. He refers to the Democratic Party's plans for America as "bizarre and destructive," a "nightmare vision for America."

Mr. Hannity calls the Democrats' Green New Deal "the granddaddy" of these plans. The GND is a congressional resolution introduced by Representative Alexandria Ocasio-Cortez of New York and Senator Edward J. Markey of Massachusetts. The resolution presents a complex plan for tackling climate change, calling on the federal government to wean the United States from fossil fuels and curb greenhouse gas emissions.

Mr. Hannity questions the Left's true objectives behind the GND. He quotes Ms. Ocasio-Cortez' former chief of staff, Saikat Charkrabati as saying, "Do you guys think of it [the GND] as a climate thing? Because we really think of it as a how-do-you-change-the-entire-economy thing."

Other leftists agree. In the *New York Magazine* section called *Curbed*, writer Diana Budds said the GND "is really about designing an entirely new world." Environmentalist Bill McKibben said the GND is "a change to address not only rising temperature but the rising inequality that roils our politics ... Ideas like a federal job guarantee for anyone who wants to help with the renewables transition are important precisely because they give people a chance to get their feet on the ground." Put that way, the GND starts to sound like another Welfare program and will, in fact, cost the U.S. taxpayer trillions of dollars.

Sean Hannity wrote, "The Green New Deal is horrifying, ambitious, reckless, and fiscally incoherent. But it cannot be dismissed as some pie-in-the-sky leftist fantasy because Democrats are dead serious about it."

What's Next for America?

There can be no doubt that we, like our allies in Europe, are now letting socialism gain traction in our own country. Mr. Scaliger's studies convinced him of the same things we can observe with our own eyes. The United States has entered the phase of "socialist degradation," which is a "near-universal prelude to the barbarities of totalitarianism that will eventually follow."

Yet, money must remain the focus and the goal. Since socialism can't produce enough wealth on its own, it must be combined with a corrupt version of capitalism. Though clearly injurious, fraudulent, and unjust, the liberals in Congress will never allow the economic drains to be plugged. They profit too much by trading on the misery of the poor. As the Communists use the "proletariat" working class, American politicians use the poor as a device to assume and retain power. Since anti-poverty programs in the U.S. have actually increased poverty, left-leaning politicians have an even broader base of support for their merger of capitalism and socialism.

Sad to say, the die is cast. Until its final demise, the American economy is destined to be an unholy mixture of philosophies espousing material blessings on the one hand and altruistic welfare on the other. ■

Chapter 7
The Humanist Economy Welcomes the Antichrist

In spite of the hatred and ideological struggles between capitalism and socialism, the two manage to intermingle in most twenty-first century societies. Given the recent financial meltdown, as well as the results of the presidential election, all of that is about to change.

Socialists despise private enterprise and are not content with a mixture of philosophies. To remedy the world's ills, they feel that nothing less than the death of capitalism and complete redistribution of the world's wealth will correct the mammoth inequities in today's economic structures. Likewise, humanists view capitalism as an obstacle to human progress.

The stage is set for a final end-time clash between the world's two economic forces. Considering the passion and overwhelming political clout of today's liberal-socialist-humanists, they are bound to win the struggle. The evolutionary process that began in the early 1900s will end with a final coup de grâce. At the close of the current era, socialism will totally envelop capitalism. All remaining privately-owned institutions will collapse and be replaced with international state-owned institutions.

In *Globalism: America's Demise*, noted authority William Bowen said, "The complete takeover will come through an economic catastrophe. Most likely, it will be the result of a bankruptcy of the United States government. That will trigger a devaluation of money and lead to a stock market crash. This will bring on a world depression—and a global government which will be thought necessary to solve all our problems."

The socialist machinery is in place, with some version of socialism already controlling or influencing almost every major world government. As soon as the massive financial collapse takes place, a powerful leader will arise to organize the confused, national economies into a universal system. Naturally, this system will include no modicum of private ownership or personal liberty.

Covetous Socialism

Recipients of redistributed income are coveting other people's money, the goods of the more productive members of society, and the Bible clearly shows that covetousness is a sin. To even contemplate seizing someone else's possessions for our own use is a sin. Consider how grave the sin must be if one actually votes to confiscate his neighbor's goods (his income), knowing that the money will be doled back out to you.

When morals disintegrate and self-gods vote themselves a paycheck, capitalism is destined to fall. Humanism exploits the dark side of democracy, disposing of all incentive to excel, to improve oneself, or to seek just rewards for superior talent, energy, or skill. Working as the redistribution team, humanism and democracy degrade the profit-driven apparatus to a mere support mechanism, until it is finally dissolved by the state.

Taxation without Representation

Some call it economic justice. It may, in fact, be more closely akin to extortion or highway robbery. In *Democracy and Liberty*, William Edward Hartpole Lecky wrote, "The inevitable result is to give one class the power of voting taxes, which another class almost exclusively pays, and the chief taxpayers, being completely swamped, are for all practical purposes completely disenfranchised." If you've ever felt helpless, frustrated or angry at tax time, you have good reason. You have been disenfranchised from the political process. You have no say in where your money goes.

For all intents and purposes today, the voice of many in America's democracy has been surreptitiously silenced by way of taxation without representation. Liberal coalitions team with the 44% of Americans who do not pay income taxes (according to the Tax Policy Center, in July of 2018), to overwhelm productive, tax-paying patriots. Our level of taxation no longer matches our level of representation. Sound familiar? This injustice was a fundamental impetus for the first American Revolution.

The Fifth Amendment to the American Constitution says, "nor shall private property be taken for public use, without just compensation." Property, according to James Madison, includes a man's land, merchandise, and money. Our money is our private property, and we definitely do not receive just compensation for our taxed dollars.

The Income Tax amendment was passed in 1912, and since then, there have been no constitutional limits on the progressive rape of personal and corporate income earners. Some today suggest a flat tax. That could be a viable solution, but only if our money would be used for the common good: deserving and productive purposes, as well as protection of our national security. At this time, that is not where the money goes.

In an earlier time, freedom and fairness were the essence of life itself, being taxed without consent or just compensation was enough for taxpayers to rise up in revolt against the heavy hand of the extortionist. Given the state of affairs in the world today, and the depths to which humanity has sunk, we fear it is too late to change the course of our downward spiral. America is destined to fail, and free enterprise will die with it.

The Antichrist and Communism

Once this happens, the Antichrist will be free to institute his worldwide socialistic state, with a regime resembling communism. Free enterprise, as it exists today, will be gone forever.

Communism, on paper, centers around community ownership of property. It requires cooperation, with each person producing according to his ability, and then voluntarily sharing with others. All of society's needs are satisfied through sharing. The intellectual elite take charge to control the economy, and presumably to ensure fairness.

According to the pure concept of Communism, the elite leaders will turn over control to "the people," once those ignorant masses are capable of governing themselves. Unfortunately, once someone gains power, they are seldom eager to relinquish it. As the elite doggedly cling to their powers, the proletariat's hope for community ownership, voluntary cooperation, and equal say in a democratic government quickly deteriorate into communist nightmares.

We've seen it happen in history, time and time again. The means of production and distribution, theoretically owned by the community, are in reality owned by the state, with workers receiving only bare subsistence in exchange for slave labor. Collectivization of agriculture and forced distribution of scarce commodities replace voluntary sharing. Democratic central governments become dictatorial states, with no proletariat participation.

The original strategy to impose Marxist Communism included written goals such as:

- Gain control of the schools and all student newspapers
- Infiltrate the press
- Gain key positions in the media
- Discredit American culture and all forms of artistic expression

Those who oppose the state are generally crushed without question. The brutal murder of millions of dissidents in Russia, China, Vietnam, Cuba, etc., attests to this grim fact.

In China, Mao Zedong led the charge to collectivize agriculture and ramp up industrialization. As Sean Hannity describes in *Live Free or Die*, Mao's "Great Leap Forward" was one of the greatest tragedies in world history. The Chinese government seized land, home, belongings, and livelihoods from the people and forced them onto giant communal farms. Based on archives of the Chinese Communist Party, historian Frank Dikkoter reports that 2-3 million people were tortured to death or killed, and overall, the Great Leap Forward resulted in at least 45 million deaths, making Mao "one of the greatest mass murderers in history."

Loss of life means nothing to a Communist. The state must be preserved. The Communist Party must remain in power and unchallenged.

Karl Marx was humane in his theories but arrogant and dictatorial in his style. He was domineering, with boundless self-confidence. Devoid of any belief in God, Marx and his friends were described as self-appointed gods. Marx even considered himself godlike and equal to the Creator, an opinion very reminiscent of his predecessor, Satan, and his egomaniacal successor, the Antichrist.

Is it any wonder that Marx's theories, when put into practice, produce governments that emulate the style of their creator? Marxist philosophies inevitably lead to dictatorial, atheistic states governed by self-appointed gods. These "gods" use totalitarian thought-control and brute force to recondition the minds of the masses.

This path of Communism leads to loss of life and liberty, to the perfection of slavery and inhumanity, to concentration camps. It leads to tyrannical monopolization of privilege and power by a small aristocracy. It leads to collective poverty, scarcity, production inefficiencies, and economic chaos or stagnation. Finally, tragically, it leads the world to the Antichrist. ■

Chapter 8
The Fall of New America

At one time, America was the greatest country ever to exist on this planet.

Today, the new America is bankrupt and on the verge of collapse, trillions of dollars in debt. Christian morals are a distant memory. Liberals have hastened the downward spiral with self-loving, humanistic, God-free values, and their "progressive" version of economics. Not even the COVID-19 pandemic has been able to turn Americans back to God.

The deliberate devaluation of all that was America makes for a sad story, with an even sadder ending. It is painful to look into our future, especially since we seem helpless to turn this mighty ship around. At present day, America has no resemblance to the vision of our founding fathers. Those founding fathers, men of integrity and soldiers for liberty, would have revolted long ago against this tyrannical disaster. The Pilgrims and Puritans would never consider making a landing here today, especially in a place like Massachusetts.

The world hates us and would love to dance on our

graves. Communists hate our prosperity. Muslims hate our immoral lifestyles and allegiances to Israel. Iran considers us the great Satan and feels they must destroy us before their Messiah can come. Most of us can accept the hatred directed at us from our envious enemies, but it is hard to swallow when the hatred comes from within.

The liberals go on spending, digging the debt hole deeper and deeper, with massive welfare handouts, national and international giveaway programs, deficit spending, borrowing, and printing money until the presses melt. Already, the present value of all entitlement programs exceeds fifty trillion dollars. There is no way we will ever pay for that, and our liberal leaders probably don't intend to.

Globalism vs. Nationalism

It is certainly difficult to understand and accept the humanists' aggressive attempts to destroy the very fabric of America. Why would so many of our own countrymen want us to fail? Why would they want to take the greatest experiment in human governance, personal freedoms, and economic achievements and rip it to shreds?

The Humanist Manifesto speaks of moving toward a world community by developing "a system of world law and a world order based upon transnational federal government." They go on to say that war is "obsolete" and that we should instead enact "peaceful adjudication of differences by international courts." Unfortunately, before the humanistic socialists can establish their one-world community, the mighty eagle that is America must be shot down. National superpowers can't coexist with a liberal utopia. Independent nations have no place in the New World Order. Neither do patriots.

En route to the humanist world community, America the beautiful must be fundamentally transformed into a globalist-minded citizenry. The focus must change entirely:

- From freedom to peace
- From individuality to collectivism
- From righteousness to rights
- From life to choice
- From family to community
- From distinction to unity
- From security to disarmament
- From competition to cooperation

The global citizen must think and act beyond his national borders. He is a member of the world community, no longer bound by national loyalties or inspired by a strong, independent, nationalistic spirit. Love for America has to be supplanted by the universal brotherhood of man. The global New World Order must become his new home.

To the liberal, America is just a place to live and enjoy the fruit of someone else's blood, sweat, and tears. America's blessings are to be extorted and exported around the world until there is nothing left to give away. The concept of national bankruptcy doesn't seem to bother them. They see no value in preserving the national personality, the American mission, or our position as a beacon of hope for the world's estranged. America must be sacrificed for the good of the world.

These humanists don't give us much to look forward to, just the concrete coldness of Soviet-style rigidity, black markets, and even more corrupt officials and politicians.

Considering America's historic fight with Soviet Russia and Communism, it may seem hard to believe that Americans would ever turn to a Communist regime. Even today, however, Communist forces are at work within our country. The headline on the website of the Revolutionary Communist Party (www.revcom.us) states, "Welcome to the Revolution." They go on to say, "Our fundamental goal, and guiding star, remains: REVOLUTION—NOTHING LESS!" This group pushes for an uprising, stating that we must "overthrow—not heal" the system. Their leader, Bob Avakian, supposedly has developed "scientific" communist theory "on a world-class level." In their "Six Points" he states, "We base ourselves on and strive to represent the highest interests of humanity: revolution and communism … We fight for a world without borders." Antifa is purportedly a front group for the Revolutionary Communist Party. The group Black Lives Matter, too, has Marxist ties.

Perhaps the theory and reasoning behind the globalist mindset is that the world has shrunk and so, too, must we. Accordingly, we must think in terms of a global village with a transnational federal government, world law administered by international courts, and global banking routed through the United Nations.

The Next Step for New America

Scripture implies that the ultimate demise of America will occur when all nations, including our own, are gathered with the Antichrist to fight the returning Christ at the battle of

Armageddon (Zechariah 12:3). Of course, America will be among the losers. Until she fulfills her role in Armageddon, America will exist in some form, perhaps as a barely-distinguishable accessory of the global synthesis of nations. Watch as any of several disheartening scenarios unfold:

- The likes of Biden, Obama, Schuler and Pelosi will disarm us while driving us to the poorhouse with their massive and wasteful giveaway programs.
- Wall Street will have a complete financial meltdown as the market senses the futility of limping along any longer, dragging the liberals' ball and chain.
- The Chinese will call in their loans, forcing America to declare bankruptcy.
- A successful terrorist attack or a nuclear attack from North Korea, Iran, China, or Russia will demolish a defenseless America, or bully us into submission.
- We will surrender our sovereignty without a single shot and slip into subjugation, deceived by our leaders into thinking it is the only way to go.

The fact is, an unholy people ultimately only respond to a dictatorship. Absent the Christian code of ethics and its inherent limits of behavior, humanist relativism takes over, eventually followed by anarchy. Their remedy: the tyrannical rule of a dictator accompanied by the brute force of his ego unleashed on all who stand in his way.

Absent the moral code, America is ripe for a dictatorship where the ignorant masses are manipulated by their "organizers" to accept enslavement to the all-knowing one.

This, their Anointed One, will meet all their needs, as if the means to do so are just created and not extorted from the "evil ones" who actually work for a living. ■

Chapter 9 Hope for Traditional Americans

How traditional Americans fare during our country's downward spiral depends on how much we resist absorption into the global unit, and how we, as a people, respond to the sin in our lives and the saturation of corporate sins throughout our nation.

How do we effectively deal with the sins that have rendered us personally powerless? If we choose to resist the liberal socialist domination of our nation's power structures, how do we go about it? Can we reverse the liberal perversion that has brought us down into this dark hole? Can we take our country back, so that her fall is from foreign enemies rather than internal forces? America will eventually fall from her prominent perch, but let's hope and pray that it's from without, and not from within.

Given the depths of America's sins and her reluctance to seek forgiveness, should we sit back, do nothing, hope for the best, and watch the total collapse of America? Should we play the liberal game, keep our mouth shut, take the handouts, and hide our faith under a basket, smothering the flickering flame of our resolve? Should we just acknowledge the inevitable, prepare ourselves spiritually, and get ready for persecution (and perhaps death)? I think not.

If we do try to take our country back, or at least secure a portion of the country, where men are still free, we might consider the following:

- **Waging a war of ideas:**
  While conservative ideas are far more logical and proven than those of the liberals, the mass media is firmly ensconced in the liberals' pocket. Therefore, it is unlikely that conservatives can win this war to sway public opinion.

- **Electing more conservatives to office:**
  We did this recently, and were blessed with President Trump. After Trump's presidency, can the conservatives ever win another election? The liberals are stacking the electoral deck. Mobs of welfare recipients and elitist snobs simply outnumber freedom-loving traditionalists. We are past the point of electing all the honest, patriotic politicians we need because liberals have hijacked the process. The election debacle of 2020 is a perfect case in point.

- **Seceding from the unholy union, state by state, with each state governing itself as it sees fit:**
  Constitutionally, power should rest in the hands of the states. The consent of those states made the original federal government possible. With secession, states could see their taxes go for purposes they deem worthy, instead

of supporting the over-represented class of lazy bums who have learned to beat the system.

Hope through Holiness

The humanists who brought us to the crisis state we experience today can only be successfully overthrown by true patriots wielding the power of Biblical Christianity. The watered-down version of today's religion is no match for the extremely organized, disciplined, and determined forces of evil drowning today's world in socialistic filth. A few independent voices, crying in the wilderness, will not be sufficient. America must have a sea change, a paradigm shift in our mood and morals. We need a national reformation.

The warriors in this fight must first have undergone their own personal revolution and reformation against their sinning nature. Each of us must overthrow immorality and all other vestiges of humanism. We must turn to the biblical version of holiness and rebel against the effects of liberal humanism on our hearts and lives. If the die is cast for America's future, our only hope is our own spiritual revolution.

We must solidify our conviction that the pursuit of holiness is the only antidote to the forces arrayed against us and our country. Holiness must no longer be stigmatized as a dirty word; instead, it must be sought after for its cleansing effects on the heart, a heart that has been contaminated by humanist toxins for so many years.

But, what of America? Could we somehow reform our country on a national level? If we could stage a national, moral revolution, our leaders would be honest statesmen. Our people would love and care for one another. God would shine His support on our country once again and would rebuild the hedge of protection around us.

We will not change America by mere statements of faith and doctrines. Nor will we succeed by imposing our will in the political arena. But we should continue to vote for honest patriots who love the old America and would work to revive the traditions of self-reliance and strong morality. Those were the traits that made us the greatest nation ever to populate the Earth.

The leaders we elect into office must be those who:

- Are strong enough to defend us from our enemies
- Seek justice and tell the truth
- Rule for public service and not party ideologies
- Were chosen for merit, not money or the promise thereof
- Fight for the life and rights of our unborn citizens
- Govern the nation without bowing to special interests

If we choose to reform **ourselves** and apply our greatest energies toward creating a national American reformation, we will reap eternal benefits, no matter what ultimately happens to the country.

Time is running out. We are in a war for our souls and the soul of America. It may be too late for America to be "saved," but we can win the fight against humanism, liberalism, and relativism in our own lives. Our quest for holiness must be sought with the same passion our enemies exercise against us and our great nation. ■

"Follow peace with all men, and holiness, without which no man shall see the Lord"

(Hebrews 12:14)

Conclusion

The world teeters on the brink of a cataclysmic paradigm shift in both the behavior and the philosophies of its citizens. Everything is about to change: the accumulation and distribution of wealth, the isolation and extermination of Israel, the influence of biblical Christianity, and the subjugation of the American superpower.

It is late on the line of time, but not too late for us to prepare for the dark days. We must purge the temple and proceed on a journey into the most hopeful time in man's history. The blessed hope. This will be the time that apostles and saints through the ages have longed for.

As Christians, we know tough times are coming. We expect them and accept them, but not lying down. We will prepare our hearts and minds for a holy walk before God. We will give up that which Christ purchased when He gave up His life: our own lives.

America will fall or fold before the end of time, but "we, the people" do not have to fall with it. We do not need to merge into the global humanist cesspool of immorality. We, as individuals, can rise from the ruins through personal reformation and a return to the roots of our beliefs:

Biblical Christianity.

While the world accelerates toward the cataclysmic events of the Tribulation and Armageddon, let us not forget what a wondrous time will follow: a time for those who name the name of Christ and return to the fervor and anticipation of the first century Church. Those Christians knew the Lord. They blended as one in the upper room. Their hearts were clean, their exploits were many, and their minds were focused on the soon return of their risen Lord.

Let us join with John the Revelator when he said at the end of Revelation, "Even so, come, Lord Jesus" (Revelation 22:20). And, let's really mean it.

"But as he which hath called you is holy,
so be ye holy in all manner of conversation;
because it is written, Be ye holy; for I am holy."

(1 Peter 1:15-16)

About The Author

THOMAS G. REED

THOMAS REED is a husband, father, a successful entrepreneur, and author. His love for country and Christianity evoked in him the need to take a two-year sabbatical to study and try to understand the true meaning of holiness. It was during this time that Thomas began his journey in writing.

The End of Old America, SECOND EDITION, explores the question of what happened to the America with which our Founding Fathers entrusted us and the America in which our parents grew up believing in and wanting to pass down to generations to come.

Thomas invites you, the reader, to explore with him through the pages of this book, the hope of taking back our beloved country so that our children and grandchildren will have the American heritage that was so important to our Founding Fathers to preserve and protect.

Thomas received his BA degree from East Carolina University. He is married and the father of four sons. He has seven grandchildren and is a successful business owner in Western North Carolina.

www.ingramcontent.com/pod-product-compliance
Lightning Source LLC
LaVergne TN
LVHW021157160826
845679LV00024B/2144

* 9 7 8 1 9 5 7 5 2 8 0 8 3 *